Aviation and tourism policies

CW00606762

Aviation and tourism have long been seen as interdependent segments of one single industry. Increasingly, the World Tourism Organization and its member governments recognise that developments in aviation will significantly affect the nature and growth of tourism.

Aviation and Tourism Policies makes an important contribution to the growing worldwide debate on aviation and tourism policy issues. This publication reviews recent developments in aviation, such as changes in air transport regulation, and examines the rationale behind the various controls imposed on air services and the reasons for the current radical transformation of the industry throughout the world.

A review of past and present policies pursued in a representative group of countries helps illustrate the difficulties many governments have in balancing the interests of their national airlines and the optimum development of their tourism industries. In addition, a number of simple models designed to assist countries in evaluating effective policy directions are presented.

Aviation and Tourism Policies offers an effective methodology for the measurement and comparison of the costs and benefits of policy options, and will become a vital guide to the dynamics between aviation and tourism in the modern context. It will be of importance for students of tourism management and policy-makers alike.

Aviation and Tourism Policies was developed with the expertise of WTO consultant Stephen Wheatcroft, one of the world's leading experts in aviation and tourism.

A World Tourism Organization Publication
Published by Routledge

In collaboration with the World Tourism Organization (WTO), Routledge is publishing authoritative books on key issues in tourism. The WTO is the leading international organisation in tourism and travel, and its reputation endorses the scope and quality of these projects. The organisation focuses on the promotion and development of tourism worldwide, stimulating business and economic growth and providing valuable, comprehensive data on the world's largest industry.

Also available:

National and Regional Tourism Planning
World Tourism Organization

Aviation and tourism policies

Balancing the benefits

London and New York

First published 1994
by Routledge
11 New Fetter Lane, London EC4P 4EE

Simultaneously published in the USA and Canada
by Routledge
29 West 35th Street, New York, NY 10001

© 1994 World Tourism Organization

Typeset in Times by J&L Composition Ltd, Filey, North Yorkshire
Printed and bound in Great Britain by
Biddles Ltd, Guildford and King's Lynn

British Library Cataloguing in Publication Data
A catalogue record for this book is available from the British Library.

Library of Congress Cataloging in Publication Data
Wheatcroft, Stephen.
    Aviation and tourism policies: balancing the benefits/Stephen
Wheatcroft.
    p.   cm. – (World Tourism Organization/Routledge)
Includes bibliographical references and index.
    1. Airlines – Deregulation.   2. Aeronautics, Commercial –
Deregulation.
    3. Aeronautics and state.   4. Tourist trade.   I. Title.   II. Series.
HE9777.7.W48 1994
338.4′791—dc20   93–46085
                                                                    CIP

ISBN 0–415–10987–6 (hbk)   ISBN 0–415–10988–4 (pbk)

Contents

Figures

Tables

Preface

The World Tourism Organization has long recognised that aviation and tourism are interdependent segments of a single industry. But it has also recognised that different aviation policies can have major impacts on the nature and growth of tourism, sometimes adverse, sometimes beneficial.

It is quite clear that aviation regulatory systems throughout the world are now undergoing profound changes and that the whole structure of the international airline industry will be radically different by the end of this decade. At the same time the governments of many countries are reappraising the importance of the contribution which tourism makes to their national economies. Aviation and tourism policy issues are being debated with heightened interest in many countries of the world.

The WTO sees these debates as involving issues of critical importance to the tourism industry. It therefore commissioned this study as a contribution to the worldwide debate and proposed that it should start by describing to a non-aviation audience the ways that air transport has been regulated in the past, the reasons for the controls imposed on air services, and the radical changes now occurring in the industry throughout the world. The book therefore concentrates on the aviation developments which have the most direct impact on the tourism industry and does not attempt to review other technical, operational and marketing changes which, however interesting, do not have the same kind of relevance to other sectors of the travel industry.

The WTO further proposed that the past and current policies of a representative group of countries should be reviewed to illuminate the problems which all countries face in trying to strike the best balance between the interests of their national airlines and the optimum development of tourism.

An analytical framework is essential for such studies: a methodology must be established to enable the costs and benefits of alternative policies to be measured and compared. Simple models have been developed in this study to assist countries – small and large – with an assessment of the comparative economic contributions which could be made by their airline and tourism industries under different scenarios.

In reviewing the polices of more than a dozen different countries the study relies heavily on data for the period 1986 to 1990. A practical reason for this is the ready availability of detailed information for these years in the comprehensive WTO publication *Compendium of Tourism Statistics*. A more substantive reason is that tourism suffered a severe setback in many countries in 1991 because of the Gulf War. Preliminary data for 1992 indicate a recovery from the slump of 1991, though economic recession continued to depress growth. The results for 1992 do, however, give support to the proposition that the trends of the 1986 to 1990 period are a valid indicator of the way that tourism will continue to develop in the 1990s.

Aviation and tourism must continue to work together for the optimum development of world travel. But it cannot be denied that protectionist aviation policies of the past have sometimes had adverse effects on the growth of tourism in many countries. It is to be hoped that the new mood of liberalisation in world aviation, stimulated to no little degree by a recognition of the vital importance of tourism, will lead to the adoption of policies which will increase the net contribution of travel and tourism to the wealth of the world.

The Secretary General of the WTO, Antonio Enriquez Savignac, who initiated this study, has given continuing support and advice throughout. Many other people in the aviation and tourism industries have given valuable advice and assistance in the production of this book. Particular thanks are due to John Seekings, a partner in Aviation and Tourism International, and two colleagues, Ray Colegate and David Lockwood, in Global Aviation Associates. Valuable help was also given by Chris Lyle of ICAO and Enzo Paci of WTO. Numerous other people from all parts of the world in airlines, tourism organisations and government agencies also gave information and opinions on various aspects of this study. Sincere thanks are extended to all of them.

S.W.

Executive summary

Synergies and conflicts

- Travel and tourism account for 12 per cent of world consumer spending, with air travel about a quarter of this expenditure.
- Spending on international air fares and receipts from international tourism have both increased at twice the rate of world GDP over the past twenty years.
- Air arrivals account for more than 70 per cent of tourist arrivals in at least twenty major tourism countries.
- Despite the synergies there can be conflicts between aviation and tourism policies, particularly if the protection of a national airline restricts the growth of tourist traffic.

Essentials of aviation regulation

- The Chicago Convention of 1944 enshrined the principles of air space sovereignty, equal opportunities, non-discrimination and the right of countries to designate national airlines to operate air services.
- The Chicago Conference failed to reach agreement on the multilateral exchange of traffic rights and, consequently, hundreds of bilateral air service agreements were subsequently negotiated.
- The basic objective of these bilateral agreements has been to protect a variety of national interests, including the promotion of trade, defence considerations and national pride.
- Domestic services have usually been regulated by a licensing system and 'cabotage' rights within each country have been reserved exclusively for national airlines.

- Bilateral agreements regulating international air services normally specify the routes to be operated, the nationally owned airlines to be designated for those routes, the capacity which may be provided and the tariffs to be charged.
- Bilateral agreements are often supplemented by 'confidential memoranda of understanding' which are more restrictive than the published agreements.
- Charter operations are not normally regulated by bilateral agreements and have been relatively free from capacity and tariff constraints.

The changing aviation industry

- The regulatory system and the structure of the airline industry throughout the world are both currently undergoing profound changes.
- Many countries are now recognising the economic importance of tourism and are liberalising aviation policies which inhibit visitor traffic.
- The widespread adoption of a philosophy of 'economic disengagement' is leading to the reduction of regulation in many industries and domestic air transport operations have been deregulated in many countries as part of this policy.
- The European Union agreed a 'Third Package' of air transport liberalisation, effective on 1 January 1993, which has radical implications for the future structure of European airline operations.
- Under the Third Package, European airlines will be able to use the 'right of establishment' to create pan-European networks.
- There is a worldwide movement away from state ownership of airlines and privatisation policies are being pursued in at least forty countries.
- Privatisation will contribute to the elimination of protectionism in international aviation policies by removing purely financial considerations from government policy-making.
- A major reason for concentration in the industry is that large airlines enjoy great advantages in marketing and are able to establish dominant positions in national and world markets.
- The process of concentration in the airline industry will continue and accelerate through the negotiation of mergers and international alliances.

- Technical developments in highly sophisticated and very expensive computer booking systems and communications systems will strengthen the market positions of very large airlines.
- The previously entrenched proposition that airlines must be 'substantially owned and effectively controlled' by nationals of the state designating them is beginning to crumble.
- There are now as many as twenty-five airlines in various countries with substantial foreign ownership.
- Liberalisation, privatisation, acceptance of foreign ownership and transnational mergers will lead to the creation of truly multinational airlines operating on a worldwide basis.
- The globalisation of the airline industry will create powerful pressures for a multilateral agreement to replace bilaterals and to liberalise entry into aviation markets throughout the world.
- In an industry dominated by a small number of mega-carriers, smaller airlines will find new roles as feeder airlines and as niche operators, particularly those with a commitment to the development of special tourist markets.
- The dichotomy between scheduled services and inclusive tour charter operations, which has characterised the European market in the past, will disappear under the Third Package.
- These changes in the aviation industry have profound implications for the future policies of all countries concerned with the development of tourism.

The objectives of tourism policies

- An evaluation of the consequences of alternative aviation and tourism policies must start from a clear definition of objectives.
- The economic objectives of tourism policies are paramount and involve the growth of national incomes, employment, foreign exchange earnings, regional development and government tax revenues.
- The work of WTO in the development of a Standard Industrial Classification of Tourism Activities is vitally important for more effective measurement of the contribution of tourism to national economies.
- The development of tourism is often a fast track for economic growth and an increase in employment.
- Tourism is often the most effective way (or even the only way)

for developing countries to increase foreign exchange earnings essential to pay for imports.

- Foreign exchange earnings must be measured in net terms after deducting the 'leakages' arising from imports required to meet tourist needs.
- More research is needed on the subject of import leakages but the currently available data show that they range from 56 per cent for small island tourism economies down to 11 per cent for more developed countries which produce most of the things which tourists need.
- Tourism can be a very effective way for governments to pursue regional development policies because, unlike other industries, the consumer of tourism has to come to the production area.
- Tourism is an important source of government tax revenues but unduly high taxes could be counterproductive if they deterred demand and reduced the tax base.

Evaluating alternative policies

- The problems of evaluating the costs and benefits of alternative policies are different for small and large countries at different stages of economic development but there are important common aspects.
- The basic issues can be illustrated by examining two situations at the ends of the range: the first case being a small island economy faced with conflicts between increased tourism development and the interests of its national airline, and the second case being a developed country which already has a large tourism industry but which may face essentially similar problems if it wants to achieve a large increase in the number of tourists.
- The policy issues faced by the small island can be analysed by considering the case of a hypothetical tourist resort called Paradise Island which attracts about 150,000 visitors a year.
- A protectionist aviation policy (including a ban on charters) ensures that the national airline, Air Paradise, carries half of the island's tourists.
- The gross receipts from tourism are $186 million a year, compared with gross earnings of $76 million from Air Paradise – a ratio of 71 per cent to 29 per cent.
- The leakages of foreign exchange in airline operations are, however, much larger than those in tourism activities, and the net

foreign exchange receipts are $128 million for tourism and $26 million for Air Paradise, a ratio of 83 per cent to 17 per cent.

- The greater economic importance of tourism compared with airline operations is also evident in the employment figures, which show that tourism is providing 8,250 jobs, compared with 650 in the airline.
- The comparative economic roles of tourism and aviation in a larger and more developed country are analysed by measuring the foreign exchange earnings and increased employment arising from policies designed to attract an additional million visitors.
- In gross terms increased visitor spending is $1,000 million, compared with increased national airline revenues of $600 million, a ratio of 62 per cent to 38 per cent.
- Import leakages for both tourism and airline operations are lower than those for Paradise Island but the net foreign exchange earnings are $900 million for tourism and $360 million for the national airline, a ratio of 71 per cent to 29 per cent.
- The employment implications involve an even larger difference; an investment of $150 million (the price of a B747) generates 400 new jobs in the national airline, compared with over 1,500 direct and a further 2,250 indirect jobs in tourism.
- The evaluations of both cases illustrate the greater economic contribution of tourism development compared with airline operations.
- The assumptions used in these evaluations for costs and operating parameters are intended primarily to demonstrate the methodology; any country can make an analysis of its own situation by substituting its own numbers into the appropriate equations.

Some case studies

- The case studies are based mainly on data for 1986 to 1990 because the Gulf War and economic recessions distorted the results for 1991 and 1992.
- Growth rates from 1986 to 1990 varied enormously and range from an increase of 131 per cent (Turkey) to a drop of 44 per cent (Brazil).
- The tourism and aviation policies of twelve countries are reviewed to find explanations for high and low rates of growth.
- The case studies fall into five categories: (1) liberalisation

successes, (2) lingering protectionism, (3) charter booms, (4) charter bans, and (5) evolving policies.

- Australia and Mexico typify those countries which have adopted liberalised aviation policies in the belief that the tourism benefits will be greater.
- Tourism in Egypt and Thailand has also benefited from liberalised aviation policies.
- Brazil is an example of a country which has maintained restrictive aviation regulation and where tourism has suffered.
- Other countries in Latin America and Africa have also maintained restrictive aviation policies without regard for the development of tourism.
- Two countries – Turkey and the Dominican Republic – have achieved very high tourism growth rates by allowing unrestricted operations by charter services but in both the average daily spend of visitors is relatively low.
- Two other countries – the Seychelles and Mauritius – have banned charter operations to protect their national airlines but in both cases the net foreign exchange earnings of the airlines are much lower than the gains from tourism.
- The policies of four other countries – Kenya, India, Cyprus and South Africa – are reviewed as examples of countries searching for the right balance between their tourism and aviation interests.
- In Kenya there is a conflict between restrictive controls on scheduled services and more liberal authorisation of charter services with questionable results for foreign exchange earnings.
- India claims to have an 'open skies' aviation policy but maintains capacity controls which have limited the growth of international tourist arrivals.
- Cyprus is engaged in a policy debate about the future of scheduled and charter services and the impact on tourism earnings.
- South Africa sees the prospect of a large increase in tourists in a new political climate and is adopting a more liberal scheduled service policy to boost this traffic while at the same time maintaining controls on charter operations.

Conclusions

- All countries need to make a systematic evaluation of the economic benefits from increased tourism arising from the adoption of more liberal aviation policies.

- More statistical data are required about the economic contribution to tourism, value added, import leakages, average daily tourist expenditure and government revenues from tourism.
- Even with incomplete data it is possible for governments to make useful evaluations of the implications for tourism of alternative aviation policies, using the framework developed in this book.
- A continuing problem in many countries is that tourism has a lower ranking than aviation in the governmental hierarchy and, moreover, tourism business interests are not well represented.
- Tourism must be accorded a status in policy-making commensurate with the importance of the industry in the national economy to ensure that the proper balance is found between the interests of the aviation and tourism sectors.

Chapter 1

Synergies and conflicts

Air transport and tourism are integral parts of the same travel and tourism industry which is now a major sector, and a growing sector, of the economies of many countries of the world. The travel and tourism industry is difficult to define and measure because it is an amalgam of activities which are associated with many other industrial sectors. There is much debate on how best to measure tourism activities but a broad assessment can be made which establishes the perspective for the present study. It is estimated that the gross output of travel and tourism (in terms of total sales) is over 12 per cent of world consumer spending and that, of this industry total, at least a quarter is attributable to the purchase of airline tickets. Air transport is thus a very important part of the tourism industry.

It must be recognised, however, that despite the interdependence there can be, and often are, conflicts between aviation and tourism policies. Conflicts most often arise when aviation policies are designed to protect the commercial and financial interests of national airlines in ways which reduce the potential of tourist travel and its economic benefits. The primary objective of this study is to analyse such conflicts and to measure the consequences of antagonistic policies. But the first step is to review the development of air transport and tourism over the past two decades to illuminate the synergies.

SIMILARITIES OF GROWTH PATTERNS

International air passenger traffic and international tourist movements have grown at similar rates in the past twenty years. Not surprisingly, both have been closely related to overall rates of economic growth. These relationships are illustrated in Figures 1, 2 and 3, which compare, first, the annual growth rates of international air traffic (passenger kilometres) and world GDP in real terms, second, the annual growth rates of world tourist arrivals and world GDP in real terms, and third, the annual growth rates of international air traffic and world tourist arrivals. All three comparisons cover the twenty years from 1970 to 1990.

Several significant facts emerge from these comparisons. The most obvious is the similarity of the growth pattern of air travel and tourism movements. It is also clear that both are closely correlated with the level of economic activity. They increase most rapidly when economic growth is fastest and are slowed down dramatically in periods of recession. The oil-price related recessions of 1974–5 and 1980–1 were both periods in which air travel and international tourism showed their lowest growth rates. And the International Air Transport Association (IATA) and the World Tourism Organization (WTO) reported adverse effects on travel in the economic recession of the early 1990s.

If price changes and other factors are disregarded, a comparison solely between international tourist expenditures and world GDP can be used as a crude measure of the income elasticity of demand for international travel. Such a comparison is made in Figure 4, which shows the growth of world GDP, international tourism receipts and international air passenger revenues from 1970 to 1990. It shows that both tourism expenditures and air travel expenditures have increased at twice the rate of world GDP, thus giving a crude income elasticity coefficient of 2.0. It is interesting to note that tourism receipts suffered more than air fares in the recession of the early 1980s.

Air travel has now gained a very high percentage share of total international arrivals for many countries. WTO statistics for individual countries show that, of countries with over a million international tourist arrivals in 1990, the twenty listed in Table 1 had 70 per cent or more of arrivals by air. Ten of these countries (Australia, Bahamas, the Dominican Republic, Japan, New Zealand, the Philippines, Puerto Rico, Taiwan and the US Virgin Islands) reported that virtually all international arrivals were by air. The relative importance of air travel on a regional basis is illustrated in Figure 5, which, from WTO statistics, shows the percentage of total international tourist arrivals by air in six different parts of the world. The relatively low figure for Europe is explained later.

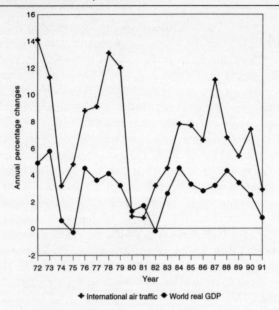

Figure 1   International air traffic and real GDP
Sources: International Civil Aviation Organization; United Nations.

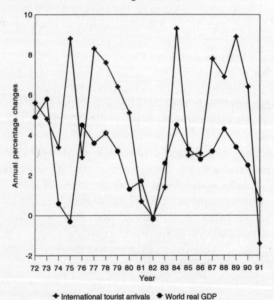

Figure 2   International tourist arrivals and real GDP
Sources: World Tourism Organization; United Nations.

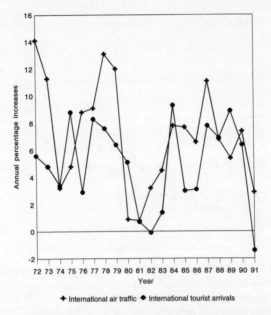

Figure 3   International air traffic and international tourist arrivals
Source: International Civil Aviation Organization; World Tourism Organization.

REGIONAL GROWTH RATES

A vitally important feature of the changing pattern of travel and tourism over the past twenty years is the dramatic increase in the share of the countries in the Asia/Pacific region. WTO statistics show that arrivals in East Asia and the Pacific increased their share of world arrivals from 3.0 per cent in 1970 to 11.5 per cent in 1990. Arrivals in the area increased more than tenfold over the period. International aviation statistics show the same kind of change. Airlines registered in the Asia/Pacific region increased their share of world air traffic from 13 per cent in 1970 to 33 per cent in 1992. Forecasts from IATA predict that this share will continue to increase and will reach 40 per cent by 2000.

All these statistics about the growth rates of air traffic and tourist arrivals raise the question of the causal relationship between the developments and the extent to which air transport has actually been responsible for the growth of tourism.

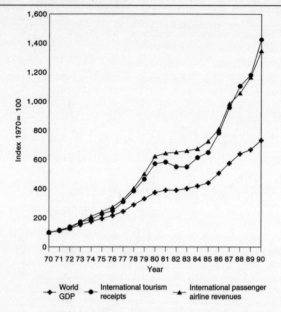

Figure 4   Income elasticity of demand for tourism and air travel
Sources: World Tourism Organization; International Civil Aviation Organization;
United Nations.

TRANSPORT AND TOURISM IN EUROPE

The development of tourism in Europe provides some answers to the
question just posed. Europe's share of world tourist arrivals has
fallen from 70.8 per cent in 1970 to 63.6 per cent in 1990.
Nevertheless, Europe remains by far the largest region for tourist
arrivals. It is, of course, true that the geopolitical fragmentation of
Europe requires many relatively short trips to cross a frontier and
thus boost the international statistics. But it is also true that
Europeans have a high propensity to travel.

Air travel, as shown in Figure 5, accounts for little more than a
quarter of European international arrivals. The predominant means
of transport is the private car, which accounts for about two-thirds of
tourist arrivals. This aspect of the European travel market is
significant because it shows that the growth of tourism is not
entirely dependent on the growth of air services: other transport
means have met the growing demand for travel.

In one particular area, however, air transport has made a special
contribution to the growth of European tourism. This has been the

Table 1 Air traffic share of tourist arrivals, twenty major countries, 1990*

Country	Air share of arrivals (%)
Australia	99
Bahamas	99
Cyprus	85
Dominican Republic	100
Egypt	71
Greece	71
Hong Kong	82
India	83
Indonesia	70
Israel	88
Japan	99
Korea	74
Mexico	70
New Zealand	99
Philippines	99
Puerto Rico	100
Singapore	90
Taiwan	99
Thailand	82
US Virgin Islands	99

* The top twenty countries are those with over one million tourist visitors in 1990
and 70 per cent or more arrivals by air.
Source: WTO, *Compendium of Tourism Statistics*, twelfth edition, Madrid, 1992.

creation of a market for air charter inclusive tour (IT) holidays. The
regulatory reasons for this development are discussed later. At this
stage it is sufficient to note that over the past thirty years there has
been a spectacular growth of air holidays from North and West
Europe to Mediterranean resort areas, so much so that these air
charter operations have surpassed the carriage of passengers on
scheduled services. New resorts in countries like Greece, Cyprus
and Turkey, if not *totally* dependent on IT charter operations, have
certainly been very much the creation of this kind of air service.

RESORTS CREATED BY AIR SERVICES

Many resort areas in other parts of the world have, even more than
those just mentioned in the eastern Mediterranean, been entirely
dependent upon the provision of adequate air services for their
development. Most of the holiday islands in the Caribbean, for

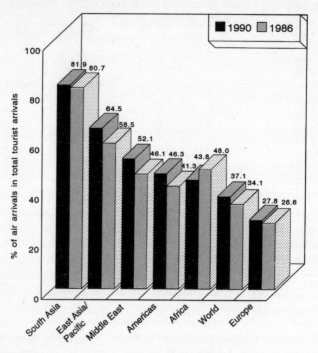

Figure 5   Share of air arrivals in total international tourist arrivals, 1986 and 1990
Source: World Tourism Organization.

example, rely entirely on airlines to bring their tourist visitors (excluding cruise passengers) from the United States and Europe. And it would not have been possible to create new tourist industries in places like the Seychelles, Mauritius and the Maldives without first establishing adequate air services. The growth of these resorts, thousands of miles from major traffic-originating markets, has been made possible by advances in aeronautical technology over the past three decades which have radically reduced the time and cost of air travel. In the years following the introduction of the first 'big jets' (B707, DC8 and VC10), followed by the 'wide-bodied jets' (B747 and DC10), and then the 'big twin-jets' (B767 and A300) the real cost of air travel was halved and so also were journey times. It is inconceivable that tourism would have grown as it has to distant destinations if passengers were still offered the fares, travel times and comfort standards of the aircraft of the 1950s (DC6, Constellation, etc.). It is in the long-haul markets that it can be truly said that there has been a causal relationship between the growth of tourism and the provision of air services, and this process continues.

POTENTIAL CONFLICTS

All of the foregoing emphasises the synergies between aviation and tourism developments. Where then are the conflicts? The answer lies in the ways that governments define and pursue their national objectives in different sectors of the travel and tourism industry. The most fundamental conflicts are those which arise from policies designed to protect national airlines from foreign competition. Such protection can lead to the support of inefficient operations, to restrictions on the services provided and to higher fares. Policies of this kind can cause a reduction in the number of tourist visitors to the country and to a loss of the economic benefits from this business. These losses may be greater than the advantages gained by the national economies from the protection of the national airline.

It is not always true that the tourism losses will be greater than the gains from protectionist aviation policies. There are sometimes reasons why it may be beneficial for a country, particularly a developing country, to protect its own national airline. And it is not always true that an increase in tourist visitors is beneficial: there are environmental and other considerations which may be negative factors in this equation. This is why it is essential to develop an analytical framework within which any country can measure the benefits and losses of alternative aviation and tourism policies and thus make logical decisions about which is best. For this reason this study now turns to an examination of developments in aviation policies, and the role of protectionism, and to a review of the rationale of different aspects of tourism policies. These are fundamental to finding the most appropriate balance between the conflicts of policies in the two fields.

Chapter 2

Essentials of aviation regulation

The air transport industry has been highly regulated throughout the whole of its history. Technical and operational standards have been strictly controlled in the interests of safety and, albeit with some further internationalisation, will continue to be closely regulated. But the economic and commercial aspects of airline operations have also been subject to a high degree of governmental control and it is these features of air transport regulation which are most relevant to this study.

This chapter is primarily concerned with the *reasons* why countries have adopted particular regulatory policies and the *means* by which those policies have been implemented. But these questions involve an understanding of the way the international regulatory system has developed in the years since World War II, starting from the principles which were agreed at the Chicago Conference in 1944.

THE CHICAGO CONFERENCE

Five agreements were adopted at Chicago and opened for ratification. They were:

- The Convention on International Civil Aviation.
- The Interim Agreement on International Civil Aviation.
- The International Air Services Transit Agreement.
- The International Air Transport Agreement.
- The Draft of Technical Annexes.

The first of these agreements – the Chicago Convention – created the International Civil Aviation Organization (ICAO) and enshrined the following four basic principles of international aviation regulation:

- *Sovereignty* Article 1 of the Convention states that 'Each State has complete and exclusive sovereignty over the air space above its territory'.
- *Equal opportunities* The preamble states that international aviation regulation must take due account of the equal rights of all states to participate in the traffic.
- *Non-discrimination* International aviation regulation must be 'without distinction as to nationality'.
- *Freedom to designate* Each state has complete freedom in designating the national airlines which will operate air services.

FREEDOMS OF THE AIR

The International Air Transport Agreement adopted at Chicago, but not subsequently ratified by enough countries to bring it into effect, was nevertheless important because it included provisions for the exchange of 'Five Freedoms of the Air' which were defined as follows:

- *First Freedom* The privilege to fly across the territory of another state without landing.
- *Second Freedom* The privilege to land for non-traffic purposes.
- *Third Freedom* The privilege to put down passengers, mail and cargo taken on in the territory of the state whose nationality the aircraft possesses.
- *Fourth Freedom* The privilege to take on passengers, mail and cargo destined for the territory of the state whose nationality the aircraft possesses.
- *Fifth Freedom* The privilege to take on passengers, mail and cargo destined for the territory of any other contracting state and the privilege to put down passengers, mail and cargo coming from such territory.

The first two of these 'freedoms', which do not involve commercial rights to carry traffic, were incorporated in the International Air Services Transit Agreement which was subsequently ratified by ninety-five states and therefore has very wide applicability in international aviation regulation.

The other three 'freedoms', and one other which will be described later, might more appropriately be called the 'national rights' which states bargained to exchange in bilateral air service agreements after the failure to agree a multilateral exchange.

BILATERAL AIR SERVICE AGREEMENTS

The Chicago Conference had hoped, but failed, to reach agreement on the multilateral exchange of rights to operate air services. The exchange of traffic rights therefore became an issue to be dealt with on a bilateral basis between states. Two years after the Chicago Conference, the Bermuda Agreement was reached

Table 2 Provisions in bilateral air transport agreements: ICAO sample format

Heading	Coverage
Date of agreement	Effective date Termination date Notice period
Administrative clauses	Designation (single or multiple) User charges Aviation security Accident investigation
Application of laws	National laws Settlement of disputes
Customs duties and taxes	Exemptions
Tariff clause	Scope Tariff establishment Tariff control process Arbitration
Capacity clause	Type of capacity control Significant elements
Grant of rights	Overflight and technical stops Scheduled services Non-scheduled services All cargo operations
Route conditions	Additional traffic points Omission of points Stopover conditions Geographical restrictions Diplomatic notes on route exchange
Route exchange	Homeland points to be served Intermediate points Points beyond

Source: ICAO, *Digest of Bilateral Air Transport Agreements*, Document 9511, Montreal, 1988

between the United States and the United Kingdom which became
the standard model for air service agreements between many other
countries.

There are many variations in the contents of the hundreds of
bilateral agreements now in effect but the basic structure is
described in Table 2 which presents the format used by ICAO in
its analysis of such agreements. An ICAO publication of 1988 –
Digest of Bilateral Air Transport Agreements – summarises the
contents of 1,235 agreements under each of the headings of Table 2.
It is to be hoped that this analysis will be updated by ICAO.

Before examining the contents of bilateral agreements in more
detail it is necessary to explore the objectives of states in their
national aviation policies because these explain the reasons why
particular provisions have been adopted.

NATIONAL INTERESTS AND PROTECTIONISM

The basic objective of the international aviation policies of all
countries has always been the pursuit of national interests.
Differences in policies have emerged from the particular ways
that national interests have been defined and from changes in the
balance between sometimes conflicting aspects of national interests.
The outcome of the pursuit of national interests in aviation has been
the establishment of national airlines and the adoption of policies
designed to protect them. The arguments often advanced for having
national airlines can be summarised as follows:

- An adequate system of air services is essential for promoting the
  growth of other industries.
- Foreign airlines cannot be relied upon to provide these essential
  services.
- Each country has a right to share the benefits of carrying traffic to
  and from its own territory.
- A national airline earns foreign exchange and avoids foreign
  exchange being spent on foreign airlines.
- A national airline provides employment in an industry of high
  technology.
- There are spin-offs from aviation employment into other
  industries.
- A well established airline industry can make an important
  contribution to national defence.

- Each country's pride and prestige are enhanced by having an airline flying its own flag.

All these arguments have influenced the policies of both developed and developing states and explain why almost all countries have set up or fostered their own national airlines. Protectionist polices have inevitably followed because there are many circumstances in which the national airline (and the purposes for which it was established) would not have survived the rigours of an open, competitive market.

The arguments for protecting a national airline have been similar to those used quite generally against free trade. In summary they are:

- The national airline is an *infant industry* which requires protection until it is strong enough to compete in a free market.
- The national airline needs protection against the *lower wages* and/or *government subsidies* which give foreign competitors unfair cost advantages.
- An open, competitive market involves dangers of *instability and discontinuity* in the supply of air services.
- Protection is necessary to ensure that *employment* in the national airline is secure and that essential skills are promoted and retained in the country.

The airline industry may not have been presented as a 'way of life', to be preserved with the fervour that farming is protected in many countries, but the foregoing arguments have been enough to ensure that protectionism has been a major factor in determining air transport policies over the past five decades. The next chapter will examine how these attitudes are currently changing. But first it is necessary to review the specific policy measures which have been adopted in the pursuit of national aviation interests.

CABOTAGE AND DOMESTIC REGULATION

The application of the foregoing policies to home markets has produced two primary objectives of domestic air transport policy: the promotion of an adequate network of services and the protection of those services from foreign competition. Domestic protectionism is greatly facilitated by the doctrine of *cabotage* which was enshrined in the Chicago Convention 1944 with the declaration that each contracting state may reserve to its own aircraft the exclusive right to carry traffic between two points in its own territory. The right to exclude foreign airlines from domestic routes has been one of the most important features of past aviation policies, and the right is still jealously protected by almost all countries.

Within each country the promotion of an adequate system of air services has, in the past, been thought to require a regulatory structure controlling entry, capacity and tariffs. The underlying justification for such regulation was that, without it, the inherent economic characteristics of airline operations would lead to instability in the system and a failure to secure national interests. Regulatory policies rested on the belief that airline operations have the following characteristics:

- The conditions of supply are essentially oligopolistic: only a small number of airlines can serve each route.
- Established airlines are not protected from new entrants either by economies of scale or by effective product differentiation.
- New entry is relatively easy because finance can be readily raised for a highly mobile asset.

It was assumed that, without regulation, these characteristics would inevitably lead to unstable 'cut-throat' competition.

It will be seen later that the second and third of the foregoing arguments for controls have been challenged by the outcome of deregulation in the domestic market in the United States and elsewhere. Nevertheless the propositions set out above were unquestionably of major importance in determining domestic regulatory policies throughout the world for most of the period since 1945. There were variations in the constitution of licensing authorities and differences in the degree to which entry, capacity and tariffs were regulated, but the underlying system was based on the conviction that economic controls were essential. Regulatory systems of this kind still exist in some countries but, as will be seen, there is now a powerful movement towards domestic deregulation.

SOVEREIGNTY AND TRAFFIC RIGHTS

In international airline operations the legal basis for protectionist policies is the principle of sovereignty over air space which, as described earlier, was enshrined in the Chicago Convention of 1944. It is this right, together with the associated provisions of the Convention, that enables states to impose conditions on the operation of air services and, in particular, to require 'special permission or other authorisation' for scheduled international services.

Sovereignty and associated concepts do not preclude the adoption of liberal policies in granting traffic rights to the airlines of other countries. Nor do they preclude a multilateral exchange of rights. But they have provided the justification for the essentially protectionist system of bilateral agreements which has been the predominant feature of international aviation regulation in the post-war years.

PROTECTIONIST ASPECTS OF BILATERAL AGREEMENTS

The dominant role of bilaterals in the international regulatory system arose, as noted earlier, from the failure of the Chicago Conference in 1944 to agree a multilateral system for the exchange of traffic rights. Very few of the countries represented at Chicago were willing to subscribe to a free exchange of the 'Five Freedoms', and a particular stumbling block was Fifth Freedom rights. Subsequently another 'freedom' came into the picture and 'Sixth Freedom' issues further complicated the exchange of rights. It can be defined.as follows:

● *Sixth Freedom* The privilege to carry traffic between the home country to another country by way of an intermediate country with which there is already an agreement on Third and Fourth Freedom traffic rights. (This is sometimes described as adding together two sets of Third and Fourth Freedom traffic rights and an example might be the carriage of traffic by a Dutch airline from London, via Amsterdam, to Athens.)

As described in Table 2, bilateral agreements deal with many matters, but the essential regulatory issues are covered by the clauses which deal with five basic issues: routes, designation, ownership, capacity and tariffs.

Specification of routes

Bilateral agreements specify the routes which may be operated by the airlines of the two contracting countries, often in an annex which can be amended without changing the core agreement. The route schedule specifies not only direct routes between the two countries but also intermediate points and points beyond each country. The right to carry traffic to and from the points beyond – Fifth Freedom rights – will normally require the agreement of the other countries concerned before they can be used.

Designation of airlines

Each country is given the right to designate (i.e. to license) the airline(s) which can operate the routes specified in the bilateral. The agreement may provide for *single designation*, meaning that each state will only authorise one airline to operate on each route, or it may agree to *multiple designation*, meaning that each state has the right to authorise more than one airline to operate each route.

Of the 1,235 bilateral agreements analysed in the 1988 ICAO study, slightly more than half (629) provided for multiple designation and the rest (606) restricted operations to only one airline for each route. Even when the agreements allow multiple designation the states concerned may restrict operations to only one airline and this has been a common feature of regulation in many parts of the world. Multiple designation has been favoured by those countries which have a large airline industry and international routes of high traffic potential. Developing countries, on the whole, have been more cautious and have favoured the single designation of a nationally owned airline and a single inbound foreign airline.

Ownership and control

It is a general feature of bilaterals that designated airlines should be 'substantially owned and effectively controlled' by nationals of the state concerned. There are no internationally agreed rules about ownership and control. Many countries limit foreign equity ownership to 25 per cent and, even when up to 49 per cent foreign equity ownership is permitted, more stringent rules are applied to control. These limit the role of foreigners in the policy-making processes of national airlines.

Non-controlling foreign investments in airlines have significantly increased in recent years but very few countries (with the notable exception of New Zealand) have been willing to allow complete foreign ownership and control of their airlines.

There has, however, been a very important new development in the European Union. It is now fully accepted that the Treaty of Rome eliminates all barriers to transnational airline ownership *within* the Union. The implications of this 'Union ownership' principle for the future structure of the European airline industry are discussed in the next chapter.

Capacity regulation

Bilateral agreements almost invariably declare that there should be *a fair and equal opportunity* for the airlines of each country to operate on the routes which have been agreed. Some countries take the view that fair and equal opportunities mean that their own national airline should offer half the capacity and carry half the traffic on the designated routes. In many cases such countries have encouraged and supported pooling agreements between the airlines so that revenues are equally shared irrespective of the carriage of traffic. Such pooling agreements were once a common feature of intra-European operations but have now disappeared in a more competitive regulatory regime.

The US–UK Bermuda Agreement envisaged a liberal interpretation of 'fair and equal opportunities'. There was to be no predetermination of capacity operated by the airlines of either country. But each country could ask for an *ex post facto* review if it thought that the operations of the airlines of the other country were unduly prejudicing the services of its own airline(s). In practice the Bermuda principles of liberal capacity regulation have been severely strained and various forms of predetermination have emerged, even in the relationships between countries which profess to support this type of agreement.

Tariff regulation

The general policy of most bilaterals is that fares and rates on routes between the two countries should be subject to the approval of the two governments concerned. For practical reasons, from the time of the 1946 Bermuda Agreement, governments have agreed to delegate rate-making to the airlines through the traffic conferences of the International Air Transport Association. Bilateral agreements have therefore stipulated that, whenever possible, tariffs should be agreed in IATA traffic conferences and should then be subject to government approval. In the event of failure to reach agreement within IATA the designated airlines of the two countries should seek agreement among themselves, but again subject to government approval.

This system worked smoothly for many years but the whole concept of price control has been increasingly challenged in recent years and the rate-making powers of IATA have been eroded. The US government, in particular, has serious doubts about the desirability of price fixing and is currently considering the withdrawal of the immunity given to airlines to participate in agreements which would otherwise contravene US anti-trust legislation. The European Union has also moved towards a much more competitive system for airline pricing within Europe, as described in the next chapter, and has proposed to make tariff co-ordination illegal except for interlining, when through fares are agreed for connecting airline services.

Nevertheless many countries in the developing world still regard tariff regulation as an essential feature of their aviation policies and will not readily abandon the controls given in their bilateral agreements.

MEMORANDA OF UNDERSTANDING

No description of bilaterals would be complete without reference to the fact that many such agreements are supplemented by confidential *memoranda of understanding* between the two governments. These often have the effect of substantially modifying the regulatory regime in which the airlines actually operate. Memoranda may, for example, specify the frequency of service and type of aircraft which the airlines are allowed to operate on each route. Some memoranda of understanding cover the financial terms by which weaker national airlines will be compensated for traffic (or opportunities) lost to a stronger foreign competitor. Royalties are often agreed and these are, in effect, payments for traffic rights which the weaker airline is unable to use. Nothing better illustrates that many countries still take the view that sovereignty confers a property right in relation to traffic to and from their territory.

CHARTER OPERATIONS

Bilateral agreements are essentially concerned with the regulation of scheduled air services. Non-scheduled flights have been treated differently from the Chicago Convention onwards and many problems of definition have arisen. In 1944 the participants in the Chicago Conference thought of non-scheduled services as being special flights for particular purposes. The Convention did not define the word 'scheduled' and did not envisage the emergence of a new kind of air service which, though it was not, strictly speaking, open to the general public, was certainly operated as a regular series of flights. Such were the charter flights operated for inclusive tours, which have become a very large part of total air transport in many countries, particularly within Europe. These IT charter operations are not regulated as scheduled services under the bilateral agreements. It can indeed be said that they have flourished because they have been outside the regulatory system which has controlled scheduled services. From the time of the European Civil Aviation Conference (ECAC) 'Multilateral Agreement on Commercial Rights of Non-scheduled Air Services in Europe', which was signed in Paris in 1956, IT charters in Europe have suffered only minimal controls on capacity and pricing. And even those countries which have controlled the frequency of charter flights have imposed little or no control on prices. It is significant that in those areas, like US domestic operations, where controls on scheduled services have been abolished, the dichotomy between scheduled and charter markets scarcely exists.

Chapter 3

The changing aviation industry

THE PRESSURES TO CHANGE

The bilateral regulatory system described in the previous chapter, and the nationally based airline industry which it fostered, are now in the process of profound change. The worldwide aviation system is being transformed by irresistible pressures which will ensure that, by the end of this decade, the regulatory regime will be liberalised and the airline industry will become a transnational business dominated by a small number of very large carriers with global networks and communication systems. These multinational airlines will be free from almost all forms of economic regulation except those which, like competition rules and merger controls, apply to all industries.

These radical changes will be brought about by eight forces which are driving the aviation industry in this direction. They are:

- Increased recognition of the importance of tourism.
- Worldwide moves to liberalisation and deregulation.
- Worldwide moves towards the privatisation of airlines.
- The marketing advantages of very large airlines.
- Mergers and alliances.
- Computer reservation systems and communication systems.
- Increased acceptance of foreign ownership.
- Moves towards a multilateral system.

The changes resulting from these forces are of profound importance to the whole travel and tourism industry and are central to the future relationship between aviation and tourism policies throughout the world.

The importance of tourism

Tourism is now the largest industry in the world by virtually any economic measure, including gross output, value added, employment, capital investment and tax contributions. Moreover, forecasts from the World Travel and Tourism Council indicate that in each of these areas tourism will continue to grow at a faster rate than the average growth of the world economy, thus enhancing its position as the world's largest industry.

As will be shown later in this book, governments throughout the world are increasingly recognising the economic importance of tourism and are modifying aviation policies which, in the past, have largely been concerned with protecting the interests of their national airlines. Many governments have recognised that, if aviation policies restrict the numbers of foreign tourists coming to their country, the net effects on its economic development are likely to be harmful. This is now a significant factor in the adoption of more liberal aviation policies by countries which have been protectionist in the past.

Liberalisation and deregulation

Another factor leading to the liberalisation of aviation policies has been the widespread adoption of a philosophy of 'economic disengagement' by governments in many parts of the world. This philosophy of reduced governmental involvement in the commercial affairs of businesses became widely accepted in the 1980s and continues to have a powerful influence on policies in the 1990s. It affects many industries such as banking, insurance and surface transport, as well as air transport. The airline industry is far from unique, even though its traditions of regulation are very deep-rooted.

The deregulation of domestic air services in the United States in 1978 was the first major step in this field but it was followed in the 1980s by the deregulation of domestic services in Canada, the United Kingdom, Australia and New Zealand.

In the international field the United States has negotiated more liberal bilateral agreements with several countries and on a regional basis the European Union has radically changed the regulation of air services between its member states. The 'Third Package' of liberalisation measures adopted by the Council of Ministers in 1992, and effective from 1 January 1993, sets the Union on the way towards the total deregulation of air services. In some ways these European developments will have even more radical implications than US deregulation because the Treaty of Rome provides a 'right of establishment' which entitles an enterprise of any member state to operate with equal rights in any other member state.

Privatisation

Another aspect of 'economic disengagement' is the worldwide movement away from state ownership of airlines. Here again this is a policy which has been adopted for other industries as well as air transport. The reasons for governments to withdraw from airline ownership vary enormously. For some it is a matter of political ideology; for others a practical expedient to escape the financial burden of the large new capital investments required for aircraft re-equipment. But the reasons are less important than the fact that it is happening on a very large scale.

The extent of the movement towards private ownership in the airline industry is remarkable. IATA's Aviation Regulatory Watch Group, which produces an annual report on significant changes in the air transport industry, reported in December 1990 that there were fourteen airlines in which privatisation had been completed or was in progress, another seventeen airlines in which partial privatisation was in progress, and a further ten airlines in which full or partial privatisation was under consideration: a total of over forty airlines in as many different countries where governments were in the course of reducing their ownership interests. When these are added to airlines in the United States and to others already privately owned, it must be concluded that world air traffic in the 1990s will be carried predominantly by companies in which governments have little or no direct interest in their financial results.

In the long term the privatisation of airlines seems certain to contribute to a reduction of protectionism in international aviation policies. It is true that government ownership in the past has not been the only reason for policies designed to protect national airlines: all kinds of other reasons, including national defence and prestige have played their part. But it is a logical expectation that privatisation, by removing purely financial factors from aviation policy-making, will reduce the incentives to protectionist policies and will be a major factor in reshaping the international airline industry.

The marketing advantages of very large airlines

The most important lesson from the US experience with domestic airline deregulation is that there are enormous marketing advantages in being a very large airline. They are not the conventional advantages of economies of scale: they derive not so much from cost savings as from improved marketing strength. They are often called the economies of scope. They arise from the domination of hub operations, the control of distribution, price leadership, 'loyalty' marketing schemes and the power of large-scale advertising campaigns. Very large airlines like American, United and Delta have demonstrated that these economies of scope are vitally important in the airline business and have successfully pursued them to become even larger. The outcome has been that the US airline industry has become increasingly concentrated, with the prospect that only three or four major airlines will eventually survive.

Airlines in other parts of the world have learned from this US experience and now believe that they too must pursue polices which will allow them to benefit from the economies of scope. This is particularly true in Europe, where there is a general expectation that liberalisation, and eventual deregulation, will lead to a concentration of the airline industry in much the same way as has happened in the United States. Even though the European Commission will want to control mergers which might have anti-competitive implications, it will not want to prevent the emergence of European airlines large enough to compete effectively with US mega-carriers.

Mergers and alliances

There are several routes by which an airline may gain the advantages of large-scale marketing and the most significant are:

- Internally generated growth.
- Growth by acquisitions.
- Growth by mergers.
- Alliances with other airlines.

Very few airlines have the resources to rely on self-generated growth. To be successful this strategy obviously calls for a growth rate significantly higher than competitors' and this is not easy. If it can be achieved it is a strategy with many advantages, not least that it can be based on the 'corporate culture' of a single company and avoid all the problems associated with different ways of doing things which arise from acquisitions and mergers. Despite these advantages only one major company – American Airlines – has come out in favour of this strategy.

For most airlines, acquisitions are more attractive than mergers as a route to growth because, in the acquisition, the dominant party can set the terms by which the acquired company is absorbed into the enlarged operation. This is what happened when British Airways took over British Caledonian and also when Air France acquired UTA and Air Inter. It should be noted that both of these major changes in the structure of the European airline industry were approved under EU competition rules, albeit subject to some conditions, because they strengthened the position of the two airlines in the face of increasing external competition from US mega-carriers.

Mergers are distinguished from acquisitions when they involve two more or less equal partners joining together. Mergers are always more difficult than acquisitions because they entail much more complicated negotiations and trading of advantages. Nevertheless it is likely that there will be more mergers in the airline industry in the next few years, many of them involving companies from different countries and therefore having to deal with divergent laws and customs. But the major barriers to such transnational mergers are the restrictions on foreign ownership which are dealt with below.

Because of the problems of growing by means of the first three policies listed above, many airlines are seeking the advantages of larger scale by way of alliances. Potentially the most formidable of such agreements is that between Swissair, Delta and Singapore Airlines. This alliance aims to create a worldwide network of services which are co-ordinated by agreements on schedules, blocked space, shared terminals and other forms of co-operation. The agreement is cemented by a cross-shareholding arrangement, with each airline having a small investment in the equity of the other two.

There are many other alliances in place throughout the world. They vary greatly in the degree of joint activities but are all motivated by the same desire to achieve the advantages of larger-scale marketing. Such agreements are of particular importance to smaller airlines.

Computer reservation and communication systems

Developments in computer reservation systems (CRS) and in communications technology reflect the growing globalisation of the international airline business. They also reflect one of the major advantages of the economies of scope noted earlier in this chapter.

A few years ago there were fears in industry and government that CRS facilities would be totally dominated by two major US systems: the Apollo system owned by United Airlines and the Sabre system owned by American Airlines. There was widespread concern that the information displayed in these systems would be biased in favour of the owners and that they would have substantial unfair advantages in marketing their own services. There were also fears that the ownership and control of these two systems would enable them to charge unduly high prices for the services which they provided to other airlines.

Two developments have subsequently reduced such concern. First, governments have taken action to impose codes of conduct on CRS operations to control bias in displays. Such codes have been introduced by the US government, the European Commission, the European Civil Aviation Conference, and by the International Civil Aviation Organization.

But bias is very difficult to eliminate and it is the second development which is probably more important. New CRS systems and new agreements between airlines have diversified ownership and control in this field. Figure 6, from the Fifth Report of IATA's Aviation Regulatory Watch Group, shows the extent of diversification and collaboration in CRS systems at September 1990. Competition between these systems is more effective than government regulation in controlling bias and preventing excessive charges. Moreover, new systems like GETS provided by Société Internationale de Télécommunications Aéronautiques are specifically designed to meet the needs of smaller airlines who want a cheaper and less sophisticated system than those of the largest CRS operators.

Foreign ownership

The future structure of the world airline industry will be radically changed by transnational mergers. But developments in this field may initially be slowed down by ownership constraints. The major

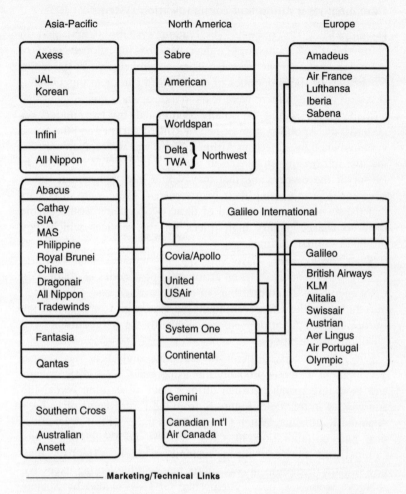

Figure 6 Worldwide structure of computer reservation system ownership: airlines and their CRS interests
Source: IATA Aviation Regulatory Watch Group, *Fifth Report*, Geneva, 1993.

barrier to the creation of truly transnational airlines is the entrenched
proposition that air carriers should be 'substantially owned and
effectively controlled' by nationals of the state in which they are
registered. But this pillar of aviation nationalism is now beginning
to crumble. Investment in airlines by foreign nationals is already
accepted in many countries, albeit with limitations, and Table 3

Table 3 Airlines with significant foreign ownership, December 1992

Continent	Country	Airline	Foreign share (%)
Europe	Belgium	Sabena	30
	Germany	EuroBerlin	50
		Deutsche BA	49
	France	TAT	49
	UK	AirUK	15
		BMA	40
		Brymon European	40
	Luxembourg	Luxair	13
	Czechoslovakia	CSA	20
	Austria	Austrian	10
		Lauda	27
	Hungary	Malev	30
	Russia	Air Russia	31
North America	USA	Continental	28
		America West	20
		Northwest	11
		Delta	10
		USAir	20
		Hawaiian	12
	Canada	Canadian Airlines	25
Latin America	Argentina	Aerolineas	30
	Venezuela	Viasa	45
	Chile	Ladeco	35
	Peru	AeroPeru	70
Australasia	Australia	Qantas	25
	New Zealand	Air New Zealand	25
		Ansett NZ	100

Source: IATA Aviation Regulatory Watch Group, *Fifth Report*, Geneva, 1993.

shows that there are now as many as twenty-seven airlines in various countries that have significant foreign shareholdings.

This development is particularly important for the future structure of the European airline industry. The European Commission has given its opinion that the restriction of European airline ownership to nationals of an EU member state are contrary to the Treaty of Rome. The Commission has proposed a European Union ownership clause for bilaterals which would extend airline ownership rights throughout the Union.

There are already, as shown in Table 3, significant developments in cross-border investment in the European Union and these will continue to grow as airlines increasingly use the 'right of establishment' to start operations in other member countries. And the moves towards foreign investments in airlines in Eastern Europe are also of significance for the future structure of the industry.

Table 3 shows that there is now a great deal of foreign investment in the US airline industry. US aviation law puts a 25 per cent limitation on foreign voting rights in US airlines and this has been interpreted in the past to mean no than 25 per cent foreign investment. This was changed in 1991 when the Department of Transportation announced that foreigners could invest up to 49 per cent in the total equity of a US airline provided that their shareholding did not give control of the company. This has led to the investments listed in Table 3, though it must be noted that the British Airways shareholding in USAir, though now approved, is subject to further review. The Department of Transportation has, however, approved the KLM investment in Northwest, which has the avowed purpose of unifying the operations and marketing of the two airlines. Moreover, a report in December 1992 from the government's General Accounting Office recommends abolition of the restrictions on foreign ownership. Of the other foreign ownership developments listed in Table 3 the most noteworthy are the British Airways acquisition of a 25 per cent shareholding in Qantas and the widespread acceptance of foreign shareholdings in Latin American airlines. All these moves are pointers towards the emergence of a transnational ownership structure in the international airline industry.

Globalisation and multilateralism

Liberalisation, privatisation, foreign ownership and transnational mergers will transform the structure of the international airline industry. As a consequence there will be great pressure to reform the international regulatory system. Bilateral agreements will increasingly be seen to restrict the development of a multinational industry and the case for a liberal multilateral regime will grow stronger.

Diminished government ownership of airlines will reduce the incentives to protectionist policies and the air transport industry will be carried along by the tide of events which is leading to the adoption of freer trade policies throughout the world. The Single

European Market, the creation of a wider European Economic Area, the North American Free Trade Agreement and the Australia–New Zealand Closer Economic Relations Agreement are all significant reflections of this tide of history. So also are the new trade agreements in Latin America such as the Andean Pact and the Mercosur Agreement. Moreover, the Uruguay Round of GATT negotiations, despite all its difficulties, is based on an agreed objective of achieving progressively higher levels of trade liberalisation.

These new pressures for a multilateral aviation agreement have led the International Civil Aviation Organization to take an active interest in the subject. It convened a colloquium on international regulation in April 1992 and subsequently appointed a task force of international experts to produce a report for a special air transport conference in 1994.

These developments are pointers to a new interest in multi-lateralism. They reflect radical changes in thinking on this subject. They would not have happened three or four years ago: free trade in the air is no longer a fantasy.

THE ROLE OF SMALLER AIRLINES

The prediction that the future international airline industry will be dominated by a small number of very large transnational companies does not mean that there will be no place for smaller airlines. US domestic experience has shown that the concentration of the industry and its domination by four or five airlines still leaves room for a large number of smaller airlines.

But the role of smaller international airlines will change, as has that of the smaller airlines in the United States. Some will form links with one of the major airlines and will provide feeder services in an integrated route network. Others will survive as 'niche' operators specialising in particular markets.

It is particularly relevant to tourism that one of the most important areas for niche marketing will continue to be the development of traffic to a home territory. An airline based in its own country and having a special interest in the promotion of traffic to that country will always have the advantage of special knowledge of its market. And, in developing tourist traffic to that market, it can identify closely with the local hotel and travel industry. The local tourism industry and the government of the country can be expected to give their support to a nationally based airline of this kind because they will believe that it has every reason to be dedicated to the promotion of their tourist traffic. This concept of 'commitment' on the part of the national airline will probably be the salvation of many small operators and may even lead to the retention of their separate identities if they are taken over by one of the mega-carriers.

THE FUTURE OF CHARTER OPERATIONS

Charter services carrying passengers on inclusive tour holidays have become a major part of the air transport system in Europe. Measured by passenger kilometres, such services account for more than half of all European air traffic. This has come about because of the past regulatory system in which capacity and tariff controls were imposed on scheduled services while non-scheduled operations were almost entirely free of such constraints.

The 'Third Package' of liberalisation measures adopted by the European Union in 1992 makes no distinction between the regulation of scheduled and non-scheduled services. The outcome is almost certain to be that the dichotomy between scheduled services and IT charter operations, which has characterised the European market in the past, will disappear. There is no such division in the deregulated air transport system in the United States and no logical reason why it should survive in a deregulated European regime. Further evidence that charter operations thrive only when scheduled services are unduly regulated comes from the history of North Atlantic operations. Restrictive regulation of scheduled services in the 1960s and 1970s, particularly through the control of fares, stimulated the development of charter operations, which grew to become approximately 30 per cent of total traffic in the mid-1970s. This charter share of total traffic fell dramatically from 1977 onwards because the regulation of scheduled services was relaxed and the market became much more competitive. Various new fare devices enabled scheduled airlines to offer prices for tour packages which were competitive with those of charter operations. Moreover, new types of scheduled service such as the Laker Skytrain took the place of services previously operated as charters.

The future of charter services in the development of tourism on long-distance routes is an issue which will be given special attention in the case studies presented later.

IMPLICATIONS OF THE CHANGING AVIATION INDUSTRY

This chapter has examined the changes which are in the process of transforming the airline industry throughout the world and the allied changes in the framework of aviation regulation. As noted at the beginning of the chapter, enhanced recognition of the vital importance of tourism to the economies of many countries is one of the reasons why the changes are occurring so rapidly. But it is also true that the changes will have profound implications for the aviation policies of many countries, particularly smaller ones whose airlines will find it increasingly difficult to compete with the emerging transnational mega-carriers. They will have difficult choices to make between different aspects of aviation and tourism policies. That is why it is essential that the objectives of tourism policy should be clearly defined.

Chapter 4

Evaluating tourism and aviation policies

The previous chapter makes it clear that the world aviation industry is in the process of profound change. The implications of the changes for tourism in individual countries will depend upon the objectives which they set for their tourism industry. These are not always precisely articulated and, when they are, they vary considerably from country to country. Moreover they may be changed from time to time in each country. The first step in an analysis of the relative benefits of alternative policies is, therefore, to define the objectives of tourism.

THE ECONOMIC OBJECTIVES OF TOURISM POLICIES

Tourism objectives fall into four main categories: economic, social, environmental and cultural. Sometimes they are also political. But, for the purposes of this study, it is the economic objectives which are paramount and most readily measurable. An evaluation of economic objectives requires consideration to be given to five major aspects:

- The growth of national income.
- Employment in tourism.
- Net foreign exchange earnings.
- Regional development.
- Government revenues.

A major difficulty in measuring the contribution of tourism to national income is defining what should be included as tourist activities. Tourism does not figure in national accounts as a separate industry: the activities and expenditures of tourists are spread over many sectors of the economy. The World Tourism Organization has been active in trying to get international agreement on how to measure tourism's contribution to national economies and has proposed a Standard Industrial Classification for Tourism Activities (SICTA) to resolve this issue. The SICTA proposal has been adopted in principle by the UN Statistical Commission and there will now be further debate and research to refine its application. The World Travel and Tourism Council has published detailed studies to assess the precise percentages of different industrial classifications in each country which should be regarded as tourism. And it has also been advocated that certain kinds of investment expenditures should be included as part of the gross output of the tourism industry. There is now general agreement that tourism activities, although they are components of other industries, can be measured and aggregated and that, for many countries, this aggregation demonstrates that tourism is the largest single component of national income.

Two other measurements of the economic contribution of tourism are important. These are the value added by tourist activities and the household incomes generated. Professor Brian Archer has pioneered the measurement of these national income factors in several reports for the WTO, the World Bank and several national governments, and some references to his and other work in this field are given in the bibliography. There is general agreement that a major economic objective of tourism policy is to maximise the contribution which tourist activities make to national income and to ensure its growth.

The employment objective is closely related to the maximisation of national income because jobs are the key to the generation of household incomes. But the employment objective of each country will be influenced by:

• The competitive use of labour in other sectors of the economy and
• The overall demand for labour relative to its supply.

If a country has relatively full employment it will be less interested in the employment potential of increased tourism than it would be if it had a substantial unemployment problem. The current high levels of unemployment in many Western countries put the employment objective higher on the priority list than it has been in past years. But it is also a high priority for many developing countries with hidden unemployment and little scope for expansion in other fields. For all countries the employment advantages of tourism development are, first, that the industry is labour-intensive and, second, that much of the employment is relatively unskilled. Investment in tourism therefore produces a higher and faster increase in employment than equal investment in other activities.

The maximisation of foreign exchange earnings is widely regarded by most developing countries as the primary objective of tourism policy. Economic development in these countries necessitates the import of essential goods and services, and these have to be paid for by exports. Tourism earnings are often the most effective way – sometimes the only way – to achieve the basic objectives of national economic growth. Many developed countries also regard foreign earnings as an important policy objective but this tends to have a lower priority in such countries because they have more extensive export opportunities to earn the foreign exchange necessary to pay for imports.

Leakages of foreign exchange earnings

Developing countries are sometimes tempted to measure the success of their tourist activities in terms of the *numbers* of visitors rather than by the *earnings* from those visitors. This approach ignores differences in the daily expenditures of visitors, which can be increased by promotional and planning policies. Moreover the gross level of foreign earnings is much less significant than the net earnings after deductions have been made for the foreign exchange expenditures necessary to meet the needs of tourist visitors. The primary 'leakages' of foreign exchange earnings to cover tourism imports arise from the following types of expenditures:

- Imports of materials and equipment for construction.
- Imports of consumable goods, e.g. food, drink, etc.
- Repatriation of income earned by foreigners.
- Repatriation of profits earned by foreigners.
- Interest paid on foreign loans.
- Overseas promotional expenditures.

It is also sometimes argued that additional leakages arise from the extra expenditures on imports for residents who have earned income in the tourist industry and the extra imports arising from the imitation of tourist behaviour by residents. But these are questionable propositions and are excluded from the analysis of leakages in this study.

The impact of the six sources of leakage varies greatly from country to country. The imports required for visitors fall as economies develop and are able to produce more of the capital and consumption goods to satisfy tourists' needs. There is, therefore, a broad range in leakages from 40 to 50 per cent for small developing island economies to less than 10 per cent for larger and more developed countries.

More precise information is needed on this subject and it is a fruitful field for further research by WTO. A collection of past studies was brought together in an article in *Travel and Tourism Analyst* giving estimates of the leakages in seventeen different countries. It is not clear whether these estimates were based on a standard definition of the imports required for tourism. Evidence from other sources suggests that the leakage estimates in the *Travel and Tourism Analyst* article for Mauritius and the Seychelles, for example, arise from the inclusion of the indirect increases in imports described in the previous paragraph. These have been excluded in the comparison of leakages of foreign exchange earnings presented in Figure 7 and this shows a range from 56 per cent to 11 per cent. It is noteworthy that the top twelve percentages are all for small island economies which cannot yet produce many of the goods which tourists need. But even though there is a wide range in the leakage figures it must be a general objective of tourism policy to maximise *net* foreign exchange earnings by reducing the losses arising from spending on imports.

Other economic objectives

Tourism can play an extremely important role in regional economic development. The overriding advantage which tourism has in this field is that a tourist, as a consumer, has to go to the place where the product is 'manufactured'. If a country wants to stimulate manufacturing industry in an undeveloped area it has to adopt measures (and usually offer subsidies) which will make it worthwhile for new firms to set up businesses in the region. This is often difficult and expensive. With tourism, however, a government can develop a suitable area as a tourist resort and create a product attractive to an appropriate market. There are many examples throughout the world of the success of tourism as an instrument of regional economic development.

Governments are deeply and inescapably involved with other

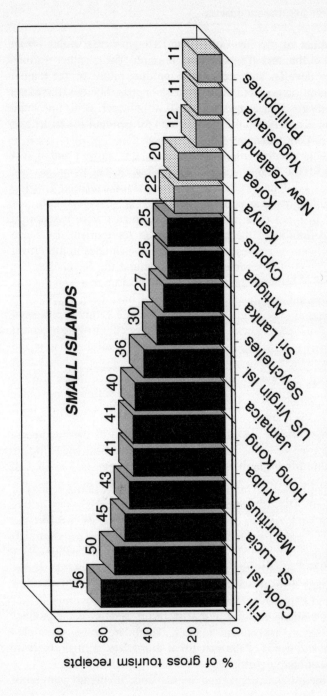

Figure 7 Leakage of foreign exchange earnings: seventeen countries
Source: Economist Intelligence Unit, 'The leakage of foreign exchange earnings from tourism', *Travel and Tourism Analyst 3*, London: *Economist*, 1992.

aspects of the development of tourism. They are responsible for the provision of the infrastructure without which private-sector ventures cannot operate. They are concerned with the promotion of tourism and normally support a national tourism organisation devoted to this task. And they raise tax revenues from tourism to meet the expenditures specific to the industry and to contribute to their other expenditures. In many developing countries the tax revenues from tourism, both direct and indirect, are a major source of government funds. The key issues in this area are the needs to ensure that tourism is treated fairly relative to other industries and, above all, to ensure that unduly high taxes do not act as a deterrent to demand. If demand is reduced, and the tax base lowered, higher taxes may have an adverse effect on government revenues.

A FRAMEWORK FOR EVALUATING POLICIES

The issues of aviation and tourism policies examined in general terms in the preceding chapters provide the basis for a systematic evaluation of the comparative costs and benefits of alternative strategies. These costs and benefits will be quite different according to the circumstances and stage of economic development of the country concerned. There is no single solution but there is an underlying similarity in the methodology necessary to analyse the situation in each country and to arrive at the appropriate answer.

The range of differences in the circumstances of the hundred or more countries seriously interested in the optimisation of tourism development is very large. The methodological approach to all their problems can, however, be well illustrated by examining two basic situations. The first case is that of smaller countries, particularly island economies, which are faced with potential conflicts between tourism development and the protection of a national airline. The second case is that of more developed countries which already have a large tourism industry but which may face essentially similar potential conflicts of policies when expanding their tourism industry.

The analyses presented in this chapter use arithmetical examples which involve making a lot of assumptions about costs and operating parameters. Although these are believed to be realistic for the situations in which they are used, they are intended only to illustrate the methodology. Any country undertaking an analysis of its aviation and tourism policies will put its own numbers in the appropriate equations.

THE CASE OF PARADISE ISLAND

The problems of balancing the benefits of alternative policies in a small developing economy can be brought into sharp focus by considering the case of Paradise Island, which is a hypothetical (but not unrealistic) tropical resort located about 6,000 km from its largest markets. It also has several secondary markets within a 2,000 km range. Paradise Island has been successful in developing its tourist traffic and now has about 150,000 visitors a year, virtually all arriving by air.

An analysis of the aviation and tourism activities of Paradise Island provides a framework for assessing the successes and failures of policies pursued in real countries with similar circumstances.

One of the objectives of the island's tourism policy has been to achieve a high average level of *per capita* visitor spending and, rightly or wrongly, it has concluded that this requires a ban on air charter operations because they are perceived to be related to low-price holidays. Whether or not as a result of the charter ban, the average daily expenditure is high by world standards and is currently $125 per day.

Paradise Island believes it to be necessary to have its own national airline – Air Paradise – to operate scheduled services. Bilateral air agreements with foreign countries are designed to ensure, through the control of capacity, that Air Paradise gets half the traffic to and from the island.

Tourism investments, operations and returns

Tourist visitors to Paradise Island, as calculated in Table 4, need 3,950 rooms. At a current average building cost of $65,000 per room in different categories, this values the investment in hotels at $257 million. Approximately 50 per cent of hotel building costs involve imported materials and equipment.

In addition to hotels, the needs of tourist visitors are met by other facilities like non-hotel restaurants, cars for hire, boats for excursions, and other miscellaneous attractions. These add a further third to the investment value of tourism plant, raising the total to $343 million.

Table 4 Paradise Island: tourism investments and operations

Hotel rooms
150,000 visitors a year
   10 days' average stay
= 1.5 million visitor nights

Each hotel room caters for
1.6 people per night
   65% annual occupancy
= 380 visitor nights per room

Hence 150,000 visitors require 3,950 rooms
Which, at current building costs of $65,000 per room,
= $257 million valuation of hotels

Other tourism facilities

These account for 25% of tourism investment
and include: non-hotel restaurants, cars for hire,
local tour operators, boats for hire and excursions
= $86 million valuation of these investments

Total valuation of tourism plant

	$ million	%
Hotels	257	75
Other facilities	86	25
Total	343	100

Foreign exchange earnings
1.5 million visitor days at $125 per day
= $188 million gross receipts

At the current daily level of spending, and an average ten-day stay, foreign visitors contribute a gross $188 million to the economy of Paradise Island. Hotel operations and other tourism activities make a gross profit of $35 million and the overall tourism business is making a satisfactory 10 per cent return on the current value of its assets, as well as contributing to foreign exchange earnings.

Air Paradise investments, operations and returns

Air Paradise has a small fleet of modern jet aircraft consisting of one A310 and one A320. As shown in Table 5 these have a capital value

Table 5 Air Paradise: aviation investments and operations

Aircraft and spares	$ million
1 A310 (210 seats)	77
1 A320 (140 seats)	40
Total valuation	117

Airline passenger operations	Revenue passenger km (million)
A310 (ten hours per day at 65% load factor)	425
A320 (eight hours per day at 65% load factor)	265
Total	690

Revenues	$ million
Passengers (10¢ per km yield)	69
Freight and other (+10%)	7
Total	76

Operating costs	$ million
Lease charges	12
Other (see Table 7)	64
Total	76

of $117 million but the aircraft are leased, not purchased. The foreign exchange aspect of the aircraft fleet is therefore dealt with by the lease charges paid out of the airline's operating account. Other airline capital requirements are relatively small and amount to less than $10 million.

Air Paradise operations produce revenues of $76 million which just cover operating costs, including lease charges and interest on loans.

Foreign exchange leakages

Foreign exchange leakages from hotel operations are detailed in Table 6, which shows the percentage of foreign exchange expenditures under standard cost headings. These amount, in total, to 40 per cent of the revenues earned by the hotels.

Table 6 Paradise Island: foreign exchange leakages, hotels and other operations

Hotels

	% of revenues	Foreign exchange component (%)
Kitchen	28	10
Local labour	14	0
Expatriate staff	5	5
Maintenance	20	10
Rent	6	0
Depreciation	10	5
Interest	2	2
Profit	15	8
Total	100	40

All tourism revenues

	% of revenues	Leakages (%)	Foreign exchange losses (%)
Hotels	65	40	26
Restaurants	10	20	2
Other activities	25	10	3
Total			31

Table 6 also shows the foreign exchange expenditures of the other segments of the tourism business, with 20 per cent leakage for non-hotel restaurants and 10 per cent leakage for other activities. Applying these leakage percentages to the revenues earned by each sector, it is shown that the total foreign exchange expenditures are 31 per cent of the earnings from visitors. This is in line with the results for similar resort areas, as seen in Figure 7.

Table 7 presents a similar analysis of the foreign exchange expenditures of Air Paradise. Each item of the airline's operating costs is shown, first, as a percentage of total costs and, second, as a foreign exchange component. Table 7 shows that 66 per cent of all Air Paradise expenditures involve foreign exchange. Very little comparable information is available in this field but the figure is probably even higher for airlines with all expatriate pilots and all maintenance and overhauls undertaken abroad.

Table 7 Air Paradise: foreign exchange expenditures

Operating cost	% of total costs	Foreign exchange component (%)
Crew pay and expenses	7	5
Fuel	15	15
Other flight ops	1	0
Aircraft maintenance	11	8
Lease charges	16	16
Landing charges	4	2
En route charges	2	2
Station costs	10	5
Passenger services	10	4
Ticketing and sales	15	9
Administration	6	0
Other costs	3	0
Total	100	66

Aviation and tourism accounts

The comparative contributions of aviation and tourism to the economy of Paradise Island are set out in Table 8. The table shows that in all three respects – net foreign exchange earnings, employment and contribution to government revenues – the national airline is very much the junior partner in the total travel and tourism business of Paradise Island.

These figures are not presented to denigrate the contribution of Air Paradise to the economy: they are the basis on which assessments can be made of the economic consequences of alternative policies, such as adopting a more liberal policy in the regulation of foreign scheduled services or removing the restrictions on charter operations.

Liberalising scheduled operations

The aviation policy of Paradise Island, as noted earlier, is based on *de facto* predetermination provisions in bilateral agreements which ensure that Air Paradise gets a 50 per cent share of traffic. Fares are also controlled by the bilaterals, and foreign airlines are effectively prevented from offering discounts. Several foreign airlines want to

Table 8 Paradise Island: aviation and tourism accounts

Measure	Tourism	Air Paradise
Foreign exchange earnings		
Gross receipts	$186 million	$76 million
Leakages	31%	66%
Net receipts	$128 million	$26 million
Employment		
Direct	8,250*	650**
Government revenues	$37 million	$7 million

 * 100 visitors create 5.5 direct jobs. Indirect employment not included.
** Includes overseas staff.

increase the frequency and capacity of their services and would, in a more competitive market, reduce the average level of fares by 10 per cent.

The most likely consequences of a more liberal approach to the regulation of scheduled services are:

- A reduction in the average level of fares.
- An increase in tourist visitors to Paradise Island.
- Little change in the nature of visitor traffic and average daily expenditures.
- A fall in Air Paradise's share of the market and probably a reduction in the actual traffic carried.

It is difficult to quantify precisely the numerical values of these developments but the probable outcome can be tested using different assumptions.

Starting from the assumption that visitor traffic will increase by 20 per cent and that average daily expenditures will fall marginally to $120, net foreign exchange earnings will be increased from $128 to $149 million, a gain of $21 million.

Air Paradise is likely to suffer financially. Assuming that it initially maintains the same level of operations, its traffic could drop by 15 per cent (from a 66 per cent to a 56 per cent load factor), and its passenger yield would be reduced by 10 per cent if the airline were to remain competitive. In such circumstances, Air Paradise's revenues would be reduced to $60 million, with little reduction in operating costs, and it would thus incur a loss of $16 million.

Even in these circumstances the gain from increased tourism receipts would be greater than the loss on Air Paradise operations. If Air Paradise adapted to the new market situation and cut its operations to match the lower traffic level, it could reduce the loss to $7 million and, by vigorous economies, might be able to return to a break-even position. But if it could not, the government of Paradise Island would have to ask itself whether it was worth while to subsidise the operations of a national airline.

The harsh reality is almost certainly that, in purely economic terms, the increased contribution of tourism is more important to Paradise Island than the benefits from Air Paradise. There may be non-economic and extra-economic reasons why Paradise Island should have its own national airline. But few of the reasons discussed in Chapter 2 apply and, leaving aside national prestige, the only persuasive argument is that Paradise Island cannot afford to be totally reliant upon foreign airlines to provide and promote the essential air services needed for its tourism. The 'commitment' factor is very important but may not justify the level of subsidy required to preserve the national airline.

An alternative to subsidising or protecting a national airline to guarantee the continuity of services may be for Paradise Island to reach a commercial agreement with a foreign airline by which the government (or the hotel industry) underwrites a minimum traffic level for an agreed frequency of services and thus ensures that air services will be maintained. A policy of this kind has been pursued with some success in the Turks and Caicos Islands and elsewhere. Such policies can be significantly less costly than those designed to secure the continued existence of a loss-making national airline in an aviation world in which it will be increasingly difficult for small airlines to be economically viable.

It may be protested that, because Paradise Island is entirely hypothetical, the foregoing analyses have no relevance to the real world. But it is highly probable that most countries, small and large, would have a better understanding of their own aviation and tourism policies if they put their own statistics into the tables presented for Paradise Island. There are many real-world situations in which lessons can be learned from Paradise Island.

Lifting the charter ban

For the reasons mentioned earlier, Paradise Island does not allow charter services and the most likely consequences of lifting this ban would be:

- The total visitor market would increase but the average daily expenditures of visitors would be lower.
- The export leakages of tourist spending would increase.
- The market share and financial results of Air Paradise would deteriorate.

The precise numerical values of these changes are difficult to assess but the outcome can again be tested by making different assumptions about each.

As a starting point it can be postulated that the market would be one-third larger if charters were allowed, thus increasing the annual number of visitors to 200,000. If the average spending per day dropped to $100 (and this is a high figure for countries with a large volume of IT charter traffic), the gross receipts from tourists would increase to $200 million. But if the export leakages increased to 50 per cent (because IT charter operators normally provide many of the facilities required by their clients in the originating country), net foreign exchange earnings would fall from $128 million to $100 million. Any losses in revenues from Air Paradise operations would be additional to this drop of $28 million in net foreign exchange earnings.

If Paradise Island were able to cater for a *very* large increase in total visitors there would be net revenue benefits from allowing charter operations. If, for example, the number of visitors doubled to 300,000 and the daily expenditure rate was diluted to $90 per day, there would be a gain of $7 million in net foreign exchange earnings. But this would have to be set against the social and environmental problems created by such a large increase in visitor numbers.

It must be concluded that there is a good case for Paradise Island to retain its charter ban unless it can adopt policies which ensure that:

- Average daily expenditures are not substantially reduced.
- The foreign promoters of IT charter operations give guarantees that they will use local products and facilities to a greater extent than is now normal with operations of this kind.

Case studies presented later in this book will compare the experience of countries which have maintained a charter ban with that of those which have encouraged this kind of traffic.

AN EVALUATION FRAMEWORK FOR LARGER COUNTRIES

The case of Paradise Island has lessons for all countries but some different issues arise in larger and more economically developed countries where the scale of tourism and airline operations is much bigger. In such countries there may be much better prospects for national airlines to compete effectively in the world market and to retain a viable share of traffic without reliance upon protectionist aviation policies.

But even in such countries a calculation needs to be attempted of the comparative contributions which can be made by alternative aviation and tourism strategies. And, in particular, a judgement has to be made whether traditional aviation policies, aimed at preserving half the traffic for national airlines, will inhibit the economic benefits which might follow from a higher rate of growth of tourism which could be achieved by more liberal policies.

Capital requirements for hotels and aircraft

The comparative magnitudes of the investments required for tourism growth in a developed country can be illustrated by calculating the capital needed for an increase of one million tourist visitors a year.

The requirements for additional hotel rooms will depend primarily on three basic parameters:

- The average length of stay.
- The average number of people per room.
- The occupancy rate achieved during the year.

Table 9 sets out some typical assumptions for these basic parameters and shows that the number of rooms required for an additional million tourist visitors is 24,800.

Assuming that a mix of three-, four- and five-star hotels can be built for an average cost of $95,000 per room, the investment required in new hotels is therefore $2.4 billion.

The additional aircraft required to bring in an additional million

Table 9 Hotel rooms required for an additional million tourists

Bed-nights required

Additional tourists	1 million
Average stays	10 nights
Bed-nights required p.a.	10 million

Room capacity

Average annual occupancy	65%
Guests per room	1.7
Annual bed-nights available per room	403

Rooms required and investment

	Rooms	Investment*
Rooms required		
10 million 403	24,800	$2.4 billion

* Mix of three, four and five-star, with average cost of $95,000 per room.

visitors, assuming that they all come by air from originating markets about 6,000 km away, can be calculated by making assumptions about aircraft size, annual utilisation and the load factor achieved. Table 10 sets out the calculations for the number of additional B747s which would be required using typical assumptions for the three basic parameters. It shows that twelve additional B747s would be required to carry half an additional million visitors. At the current price of approximately $150 million for a B747–400, the investment required for additional aircraft is, therefore, $1.8 billion.

In summary, the hotel and aircraft investments required for an additional million visitors are $2.4 billion and $1.8 billion respectively and the implications of these investment estimates are considered below.

Foreign exchange implications

As already noted, the more developed the economy of any country the greater will be its ability to provide the materials, equipment and skills required for the construction of hotels. Some special equipment may still be imported but, in general, a very large part of the investment in new hotels will not involve foreign exchange

Table 10 Aircraft required for an additional million tourists

Annual round trips per aircraft

Average distance from markets	6,000 km
Average round trip time	16 hours
Annual aircraft utilisation	4,500 hours
Annual round trips per aircraft	281

Aircraft carrying capacity

Seats per aircraft	450
Average load factor	66%
Passengers per aircraft	297

Aircraft required and investment

	Aircraft	Investment*
Aircraft required		
1 million (281 297)	12	$1.8 billion

* Assuming current price of B747–400 at $150 million.

expenditure. If money is borrowed from abroad to finance hotel construction the costs of servicing such loans are included in the annual operating costs of the sector. The capital expenditures themselves are unlikely to involve more than 10 per cent of the total investment in new hotels.

The position is quite different for investments in new aircraft. Only a handful of countries have any significant aircraft manufacturing capacity and, for almost all countries, an investment in new aircraft involves either a 100 per cent foreign exchange expenditure or a large annual leasing payment in a foreign currency.

Under traditional bilateral policies half the additional aircraft capacity required for the additional million visitors can be expected to be provided by foreign airlines. But the scale of the foreign exchange investments required for new aircraft is an increasingly significant factor in persuading the governments of many countries that there are substantial financial advantages in more liberal aviation policies. These may lead to a reduction in the share of traffic carried by their own airlines but it may be more than compensated for by the increased earnings of the hotel sector.

There are also foreign exchange implications in the operating accounts of the hotel and airline sectors. A major difference between developed countries and those similar to Paradise Island is the lower degree of import leakages in both sectors. The previous chapter has already noted that the import leakages are significantly lower in the tourism sector of a developed country than in that of one with a less developed economy. This is also likely to be true of airline activities. Nevertheless the leakages are still significant even in highly developed countries. A study of Australian tourism by Price Waterhouse Urwick in 1988 concluded that import leakages for that country were 17 per cent of visitor expenditures and 45 per cent of Qantas revenues. There are very few countries in which tourism leakages are lower than 10 per cent and it is very unlikely that even the largest world airlines have import leakages of less than 40 per cent.

From these figures a broadly representative picture can be presented of the gross and net earnings arising from an additional one million tourist visitors to a developed country. Table 11 sets out the assumptions and calculations for making a comparison between the earnings of the tourism and aviation sectors. It concludes that the gross earnings from an additional million visitors will be 1.7 times as large as the passenger revenues earned by national airlines carrying half the visitor traffic. But when account is taken of the import leakages the net earnings of the tourism sector are seen to be

Table 11 Earnings from tourism and aviation from an additional million visitors

Measure	Gross ($ million)	(%)	Import leakages (%)	Net ($ million)	(%)
Visitor spending (1)	1,000	62	10	900	71
National airline revenues (2)	600	38	40	360	29
Total	1,600	100		1,260	100

Assumptions

1 Additional visitors: 1 million
  Average stay: 10 days
  Average spend: $100 per day
  Import leakages: 10%
2 National airlines carry half additional traffic
  Average passenger yield: $0.10 per passenger km
  Import leakage: 40%

Table 12   Employment in top twenty airlines, 1991

Airline	Flight deck staff	Cabin staff	Total staff	Ratio cabin/FD	% other staff
American	9,131	16,592	87,470	1.8	70.6
United	7,278	16,004	81,242	2.2	71.3
Air France	2,745	6,195	39,469	2.3	77.3
Lufthansa	3,093	8,700	49,641	2.8	76.2
British Airways	3,352	9,675	47,181	2.9	72.4
Delta	7,728	14,519	71,755	1.9	69.0
JAL	2,426	6,283	21,485	2.6	76.3
Northwest	5,660	8,761	46,250	1.5	62.4
USAir	5,322	8,384	45,284	1.6	69.7
All Nippon	1,843	3,323	13,673	1.8	62.2
SAS	1,273	2,639	21,037	2.1	81.4
Continental	3,935	5,784	33,730	1.5	71.2
TWA	2,786	4,972	29,027	1.8	73.3
Alitalia	2,060	4,374	21,126	2.1	69.5
Swissair	1,151	2,833	20,915	2.5	81.0
Iberia	1,468	3,466	29,321	2.4	83.2
KLM	1,350	3,958	25,638	2.9	79.9
Air Canada	1,571	2,873	19,920	1.8	77.7
Qantas	1,156	3,351	15,029	2.9	70.0
Singapore	848	4,095	14,219	4.8	65.2

Source: IATA, *World Air Transport Statistics 36*, Montreal and Geneva, 1992.

2.5 times as large as those of the national airlines. The assumptions made in this comparison can be changed to substitute the best estimates that any country can introduce to describe its own market circumstances. There will be variations in the results but it is more likely that such manipulations will produce results which attach a higher relative importance to tourism earnings than vice versa.

Employment implications

Another important difference between hotels and airlines is the number of jobs created by investment in these sectors of the travel and tourism industry.

In broad terms, a four- or five-star hotel directly employs one person for every room. But, in addition, employment is created in other sectors of the tourism industry and it is estimated that this amounts to a further one and a half jobs for each hotel room. An investment of $95,000 for a hotel room therefore creates two and a half new jobs.

The calculation of job creation in airline operations is more complicated and subject to substantial variations depending on the type of operation (long-haul or short-haul) and the efficiency and productivity of the airline concerned.

Differences in the employment patterns of the world's twenty largest airlines are set out in Table 12. This shows the numbers of flight deck personnel, cabin staff and total employees of each airline. It also shows:

- The relationship between the numbers of cabin staff and flight deck personnel.
- The percentage of other staff in the total.

The number of flight deck crews for an additional B747 can be calculated by dividing the annual utilisation of the aircraft by the average annual flying hours of the crews. If the aircraft flies 4,500 hours a year and crews fly 600 hours a year, each aircraft will require seven and a half crews.

The flight deck crew for a B747 is typically four members and, as seen from Table 12, cabin staff for intercontinental operations are typically three times as many as flight deck personnel. Each B747 therefore requires seven and a half times sixteen people, i.e. 120 flying personnel per aircraft. It can also be seen from Table 12 that the flying personnel are approximately 30 per cent of total airline staff. The total employment for each B747 is, therefore, 400 people.

It can therefore be concluded that an investment of $150 million in a B747 will give employment to 400 people whereas an equal investment in hotels would give direct employment to over 1,500 people and total employment to 3,750 people. This is a major factor which governments must take into account when judging the merits of alternative policies. Aviation policies which protect airlines but restrict the growth of tourism will be at the expense of increased employment.

Chapter 5

Some case studies

Having established the broad framework within which the relative merits of alternative aviation and tourism policies can be assessed, it is now appropriate to review the results of the policies actually followed by a cross-section of countries in different parts of the world. Case studies of more than fifteen countries have been undertaken and are reported in greater detail in the appendix. Figure 8 illustrates the differences in growth rates of international tourist arrivals from 1986 to 1990 for the countries studied (except Brazil) and shows that all but one have seen higher than average growth over this period. Brazil's traffic declined by 44 per cent.

The countries studied fall into five categories:

- Those where tourism has clearly benefited from liberalised aviation policies.
- Those maintaining protectionist aviation policies to the detriment of tourism.
- Those which have enjoyed a boom in tourist numbers from unrestricted charter operations.
- Those which have banned charter operations to maintain a high level of daily tourist spending.
- Those in which policy debates continue about the best course to adopt.

As noted in the preface, these case studies rest largely on statistical data for the period from 1986 to 1990. Results for 1991 and 1992 have been distorted by the Gulf War and economic recessions in major tourism-generating markets. The experiences of the case study countries in the 1986 to 1990 period do, however, throw much light on the consequences of the policies pursued and are highly relevant to future decisions.

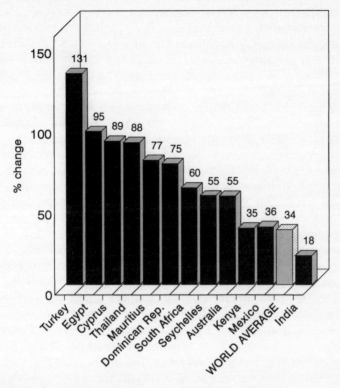

Figure 8   Growth of international tourist arrivals, 1986–90
Source: World Tourism Organization.

LIBERALISATION SUCCESSES

Four of the countries studied have pursued liberalised aviation policies for the benefit of tourism. They are: Australia, Mexico, Egypt and Thailand.

Australia

New policies recently adopted in Australia are extremely interesting to this study because they rest on a quite explicit political decision that the potential gains from expanding tourism are greater than the benefits to be derived from protecting a national airline.

The tourism industry, through its organisation, the Australian

Tourism Industry Association, campaigned for several years to persuade the government to introduce more competition into the air transport market. It had the support of an independent statutory body, the Industries Assistance Commission, which concluded in 1989 that 'travellers are denied the range of prices and services they would enjoy in a more competitive regime' and advocated radical aviation reforms.

These pressures, which pushed at an open door in the Commonwealth Tourism Department, led to sweeping changes in aviation policies. Domestic operations have been deregulated and new competition has been fostered on international routes. The two state-owned airlines, Qantas and Australian, have been merged and privatised. And foreign investment has been encouraged, with the result that British Airways has bought 25 per cent of the equity of Qantas.

International aviation policies have been overhauled, most particularly with the abandonment of the previous policy of designating only Qantas for overseas routes and the introduction of a multi-designation policy to encourage competitive services.

The key point is that all these changes reflect the very high priority which Australia is now giving to the development of tourism. The Ministry of Tourism has been accorded Cabinet status and tourism interests have been given enhanced weight in the negotiation of air service agreements. Tourism is already Australia's biggest export earner and, in the optimistic scenario, the number of tourist visitors is targeted almost to treble from 2.4 million in 1991 to 6.5 million in 2000.

Mexico

The regulation of air services between Mexico and the United States is a central policy issue because these services carry a very large percentage of the country's tourist visitors. For many years foreign airlines were only allowed to operate to Mexico City and traffic to other destinations was carried on domestic air services. This has now radically changed and there are direct international services to seven other destinations, including Cancun, which is served by ten foreign and two Mexican airlines.

The 1988 bilateral agreement between Mexico and the United States was a landmark in the liberalisation of aviation policies. It reflected the recognition by Mexico of the economic importance of

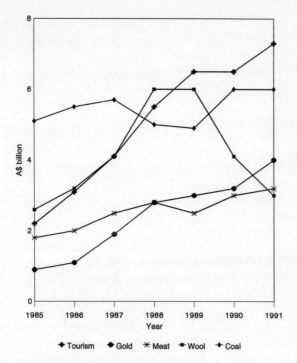

Figure 9   Australian export earnings, 1985–91
Source: Australian Government, *Australia's Passport to Growth*, Canberra, 1992.

increasing tourist visitors from the United States. The new
agreement provided new opportunities for US and Mexican air
services by a route-splitting system which effectively allowed
multiple designation of airlines on many routes.

A new Mexico–US bilateral agreement in 1991 was a further step
in the liberalisation of aviation policy. Air services are now allowed
on any route which has adequate international airport facilities and
double designation is allowed on about forty specified routes.

Mexico's scheduled airlines have been successful in retaining a
good share of the traffic under this liberalised regime. Because there
are no constraints on scheduled services, charter operations have
played a relatively small role in this market and carried only 12 per
cent of total traffic in 1991.

Mexico's experience is a good example of a situation in which
liberalised aviation regulation can be a great benefit to tourism

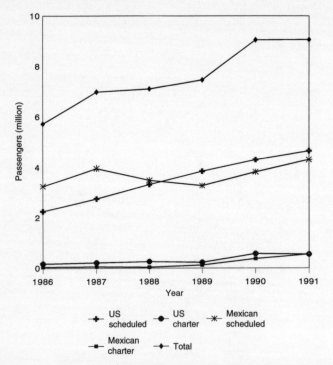

Figure 10   US–Mexico travel: scheduled and charter air traffic, 1986–91
Note: Aeromexico was declared bankrupt and ceased operations in 1988.
Source: US Department of Transport.

.without harming the operations of the national airlines of the
receiving country.

Egypt

As shown in Figure 8, Egypt achieved a very large increase in
tourist visitors from 1986 to 1990. A 95 per cent traffic growth has
been associated with a significant relaxation in the regulation of air
services and demonstrates the success of policies specifically
designed to increase the economic contribution of tourism.

Following a general liberalisation of economic policies in the
mid-1970s, Egypt adopted more liberal aviation policies in the
1980s: it encouraged competitive services on domestic routes and
invited private airlines to introduce services on international routes

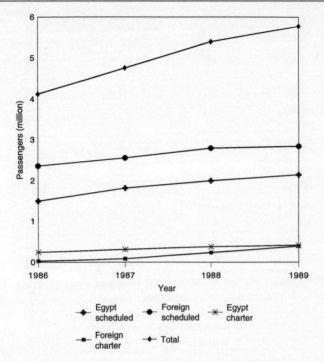

Figure 11   Egypt: scheduled and charter air traffic, 1986–9
Source: International Civil Aviation Organization.

not served by the national airline, Egyptair. Foreign airlines substantially increased the capacity of their services to Cairo.

Liberalisation has also been extended to charter services and, although these still carry only a relatively small percentage of total traffic, they have become quite important for tourist traffic to the Nile Valley and the expanding resorts on the Red Sea and in the Gulf of Aqaba.

Although there are still some bilateral constraints on international air services, Egyptian aviation policies have undoubtedly succeeded in developing tourism.

Thailand

More liberal aviation policies have produced a substantial increase in tourist visitors to Thailand. Figure 8 shows that traffic increased by 88 per cent from 1986 to 1990.

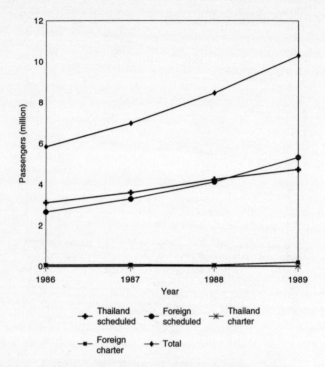

Figure 12   Thailand: scheduled and charter air traffic, 1986–9
Source: International Civil Aviation Organization.

An 'open skies' policy was announced in 1989 and the number of scheduled airlines serving Bangkok increased rapidly from forty-nine in 1986 to sixty-seven in 1991. More than half the tourist visitors come from Asia/Pacific countries and tend to be high spenders, giving Thailand the high daily average spending level of $115 per visitor.

Charter operations have been liberalised and encouraged to destinations other than Bangkok. Nevertheless, because scheduled airlines are fairly free to offer competitive terms for packaged tours, less than 5 per cent of visitors to Thailand arrive on charter flights. Future capacity constraints at Bangkok may result in an increase of charter operations to resorts like Phuket, Chiang Mai and Pattaya.

Like Egypt, there are still some constraints in Thailand's bilateral regulation of air services but there can be little doubt that liberalisation has been a major factor in the growth of tourism.

LINGERING PROTECTIONISM

Despite the worldwide moves, described in Chapter 3, towards a reduction of regulation in international air transport, there are some countries which strongly resist these changes and believe that their national interests are best served by continuing to protect their own airlines from foreign competition. Examples are to be found in Latin America and the developing countries of Africa.

Brazil

The Brazilian government has quite recently set out its reasons for pursuing protectionist aviation policies. A White Paper called *Commercial Air Transport Service Policy*, published in March 1992, explained how and why Brazil would 'maintain the principles of bilateral negotiations and agreements . . . in defence of Brazilian interests' and specifically would 'maintain the principle of predetermination of capacity'.

These protectionist policies are at variance with the avowed freer trade objectives of the Mercosur Agreement in which Brazil is a participant with Argentina, Paraguay and Uruguay. The White Paper recognises this conflict but says that Brazil will not adopt policies which are incompatible with the commercial interests of its own airlines.

The White Paper makes not a single mention of the interests of the tourism industry, which appear to have a low priority in government policy-making. The number of tourist visitors declined by 44 per cent from 1986 to 1990, which is very surprising for a country with so many attractions. It is clear that the interests of the tourism industry need a louder and clearer voice in this country.

Other Latin American countries

Five other Latin American countries – Bolivia, Colombia, Ecuador, Peru and Venezuela – have joined together in the Andean Pact to liberalise trade between them. The pact declares that they will adopt an 'open skies' aviation policy but it soon became apparent that they were not willing to accept a deregulated air transport system. Only Colombia and Venezuela, by a bilateral agreement, have made any progress towards air transport liberalisation. The other three countries continue to pursue essentially protectionist policies.

Developing countries in Africa

Separate commentaries are included later on the aviation and tourism policies of Egypt, Kenya, Seychelles and Mauritius. Most other countries in Africa, particularly some of the poorest, have endeavoured to protect the scheduled services of their national airlines from foreign competition.

National pride has been a major factor in the determination of aviation policies but many African countries now recognise that their small and often inefficient airlines will not be able to survive independently in the future. Collaboration is seen to be essential and agreements like the Yamoussoukro Declaration of 1988 have set out a programme for co-operation in many areas. But very little has yet been done to implement such resolutions.

CHARTER BOOMS

As shown in Figure 8, two countries with high growth rates of tourist visitors from 1986 to 1990 were Turkey and the Dominican Republic. Both countries achieved high rates of expansion by allowing unfettered charter operations and encouraging low-price inclusive tour holiday packages.

Turkey

The number of tourist visitors to Turkey increased by a remarkable 131 per cent from 1986 to 1990. Arrivals by air over the same period increased by 160 per cent.

This boom in Turkish tourism was mainly due to the liberalisation of charter operations and it was this sector which grew at the highest rate, with an increase of 260 per cent: traffic on scheduled air services actually declined from 1988 to 1990 and charter flights carried two-thirds of all air arrivals.

The development of IT charter services to Turkey was initially undertaken by tour operators and associated airlines in Western Europe, particularly in the United Kingdom and Germany, but the success of this business has led to the establishment, with substantial government inducements, of new charter airlines in Turkey. There are now seven Turkish charter airlines, some of which have foreign partners and/or shareholders.

The boom in Turkish tourism has undoubtedly contributed a great deal to the country's economy and foreign exchange earnings are now well over $3 billion a year. The average daily spending of tourist visitors is, however, fairly low. No official information is available but the daily expenditure is estimated to be no more than $75. The Turkish economy would clearly benefit even more from an increase in higher-spending traffic.

Dominican Republic

Tourism growth in the Dominican Republic from 1986 to 1990 was 75 per cent and, by 1990, the number of visitors was surpassed in the Caribbean only by Puerto Rico. The number of hotel rooms in the Dominican Republic doubled from 9,862 in 1986 to 20,354 in 1990.

Virtually all tourists arrive by air and the growth has been based on an 'open skies' aviation policy. The country is well served by scheduled air services but the major growth area has been charter flights from Europe and Canada.

Tourism is now a major contributor of income and employment in the Dominican Republic and the largest single earner of foreign exchange. The primary reason for its expansion is that the Dominican Republic is the cheapest destination in the Caribbean. The average daily expenditure of tourist visitors has declined as the proportion of visitors on low-price IT charters has risen and is now less than $60 per day. Like Turkey, the economy of the Dominican Republic would benefit from an increase in higher-spending visitors but this is difficult to achieve in an industry which has geared itself to low-price marketing. Attitudes which emphasise quantity rather than quality are difficult to change.

CHARTER BANS

Some aspects of the experience of boom countries like Turkey and the Dominican Republic have led other countries to conclude that they have more to gain from a smaller volume of higher-spending visitors than from the pursuit of a mass market through unrestricted charters. Two such countries are the Seychelles and Mauritius.

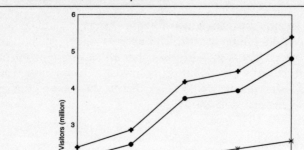

Figure 13   Turkey: number of visitors, 1986–90
Source: World Tourism Organization.

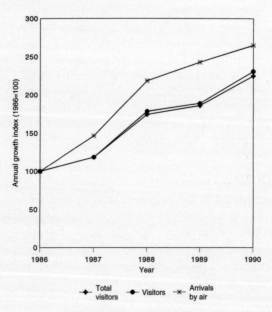

Figure 14   Turkey: annual growth in number of visitors, 1986–90
Source: World Tourism Organization.

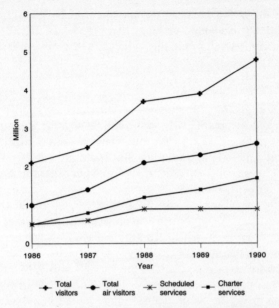

Figure 15   Turkey: scheduled and charter air traffic, 1986–90
Sources: World Tourism Organization; International Civil Aviation Organization.

Seychelles

An increase in tourist visitors to the Seychelles by 55 per cent from
1986 to 1990 was well above the world average but reflected a
policy of controlled growth and a ban on charters. Virtually all
tourist visitors came by scheduled air services and the government's
policy has been that 'charter operations will be permitted when they
do not adversely affect the viability of scheduled services'.

A major factor in Seychelles aviation policy is the belief that
tourism interests are best served by having a national airline which
is totally committed to the long-term development of traffic to the
island. Air Seychelles has been fostered, but not subsidised, for this
reason and has, so far, been successful in developing as a 'niche
airline' specialising in a limited market.

An important issue for Seychelles aviation and tourism policies is
the level of leakages of foreign exchange earnings. For tourism
expenditures these are estimated to be about 30 per cent but they are
much higher for the operations of Air Seychelles, probably more
than 70 per cent. A protectionist aviation policy which unduly

restricted the growth of tourism could therefore have adverse effects on net foreign exchange earnings. The model of Paradise Island presented in Chapter 4 is highly relevant to the Seychelles.

Mauritius

The aviation and tourism policies of Mauritius are similar to those of the Seychelles, particularly in the ban on charters and the pursuit of high-spending visitor traffic. But Mauritius has a larger tourism industry and more ambitious plans for future growth. Visitor traffic grew by 77 per cent from 1986 to 1990 and put Mauritius high in the league of growth countries.

Virtually all visitors come by scheduled air services and the national airline – Air Mauritius – is protected by the charter ban and by bilateral policies which control capacity. Nevertheless, Air Mauritius has grown successfully as a 'niche airline' totally committed to the development of the island's tourist traffic.

The major policy problem for the government of Mauritius is that it wants to retain the 'high-quality' image of the island as a tourist destination, and the high average spending of its visitors, but it has allowed the capacity of hotels and other accommodation to run ahead of demand. It may be forced to liberalise aviation policies to encourage a greater number of visitors unless it can control accommodation capacity to match the demands of high-spending visitors.

SOME EVOLVING POLICIES

Many countries have yet to find the right balance between their aviation and tourism policies and have not yet decided how best to react to the dramatic changes which are transforming the world airline industry. The current policy debates in four countries – Kenya, India, Cyprus and South Africa – throw interesting light on arriving at an optimal balance.

Kenya

The growth of tourist visitors to Kenya from 1986 to 1990 was only about the world average but tourism is, nevertheless, very important to the economy of the country.

There has been a conflict in aviation policy between restrictive bilateral controls on scheduled services and more liberal authorisation of charter services. The regulation of scheduled services remains essentially 'predeterministic' and is designed to protect the national airline, Kenya Airways. But Kenya Airways and other scheduled airlines have had to face increasing competition from charter flights which have been allowed easy access to Mombasa. The result has been that Kenya Airways' scheduled traffic has remained static and foreign scheduled services have declined. Kenya Airways has only a small charter operation and the only real growth has been in foreign charter traffic.

There is little doubt that 'beach only' passengers on foreign charter services have contributed much less to the economy of Kenya than 'safari' passengers carried on scheduled services. Moreover the 'safari' market is a more stable long-term basis for developing Kenya's tourist traffic: the country's wild-life attractions are almost unique whereas the beaches compete with equally attractive resorts in many other parts of the world. Moves towards

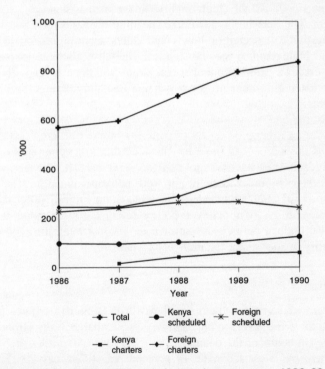

Figure 16 Kenya: scheduled and charter air passengers, 1986–90
Source: International Civil Aviation Organization.

the privatisation of Kenya Airways and/or a partnership with a foreign airline may lead to the liberalisation of scheduled service regulation. There may also be a move to a requirement that the promoters of IT charters should guarantee that their clients spend a specified minimum in the country.

India

The growth of tourist arrivals in India has been well below the world average: visits increased by only 18 per cent from 1986 to 1990. The volume is large, with 1.7 million visitors in 1990, but, relative to India's size, the country's international tourist traffic is disproportionately small.

Aviation policy is equivocal: an 'open skies' policy was announced in 1991 but it is far from being that. Domestic deregulation has been promised but little has yet happened in that field. And international scheduled services are still closely regulated and capacity controlled.

The regulation of charter services has been liberalised to some extent. The licensing system has been simplified and services can be authorised to the major cities. There is, however, an important new rule which requires the operators of charter services to guarantee that each IT passenger will spend about $50 per day in India and stay for a minimum of seven days. These provisions ensure that charter passengers make a specific contribution to the Indian economy and they also give some protection to Air India by preventing a large diversion of overseas Indian traffic to charters.

The government of India has declared that it is committed to the liberalisation of international scheduled services. It will encourage new international routes but it will continue to look after the commercial interests of Air India on existing routes. More radical changes in aviation policy are only likely to be accepted if the tourism industry is more persuasive in demonstrating the economic benefits of increasing the number of visitors.

Cyprus

Cyprus achieved a growth of 89 per cent in tourist visitors from 1986 to 1990, with a major increase in IT charter traffic from the United Kingdom and other Western European countries. In 1990 charter flights carried over 40 per cent of all air arrivals. These

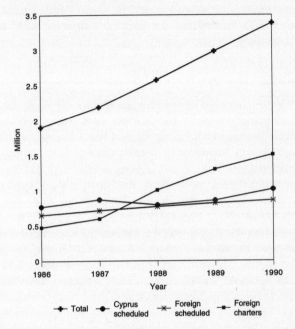

Figure 17   Cyprus: scheduled and charter air passengers, 1986–90
Source: International Civil Aviation Organization.

charter operations were almost entirely undertaken by foreign airlines: the national airline – Cyprus Airways – carried more than half the scheduled traffic but very little of the charter traffic.

There is now concern in the tourism industry in Cyprus about the consequences of these aviation developments. The tourism sector has benefited from increased traffic brought in by charters but it has also suffered from downward pressure on income because the foreign tour promoters have established a dominant position in the market and are able to bargain for lower prices. There is also a concern that foreign tour operators do not necessarily have a long-term commitment to Cyprus tourism and might switch to other resort areas if they saw advantages in so doing. This has led to new thinking about the future of Cyprus Airways.

If Cyprus becomes a member of the European Union, which it has applied to join, its future aviation policy will be determined by the

'Third Package' of liberalisation measures which became effective in 1993. The distinction between scheduled and charter services is likely to diminish or disappear and it seems likely that Cyprus Airways would be obliged to seek an alliance with another European airline.

South Africa

Radical political changes and the ending of sanctions are transforming the prospects for tourism to South Africa and the government has moved towards more liberal aviation policies to assist such growth. Domestic operations have been deregulated and, in the international field, the government has said that its future bilaterals will be based on multiple designation, the elimination of capacity restrictions and the abolition of tariff controls.

South Africa will, however, maintain controls on charter operations. Charter flights will be limited to a maximum of 400 flights a year or no more than 10 per cent of the number of scheduled flights. The declared objective of these restrictions is to ensure that South Africa does not become 'a cheap charter area' but 'promotes itself as a quality destination'.

Chapter 6

Conclusion

Air transport is a vitally important part of the total travel and tourism industry, and air services have played a major role in the growth of tourism in many parts of the world. Air traffic and tourist travel are both highly sensitive to general economic conditions and the growth rates of both are conditioned by overall economic growth. But both have a high income elasticity and both have grown at approximately twice the rate of world GDP growth over the past twenty years. In the twenty countries with more than one million tourist visitors in 1990, more than 70 per cent of all tourists arrived by air. In some places new tourist resorts have been created by the provision and promotion of air services.

Nevertheless the air transport business has been highly regulated over this period and, indeed, for all of its history. Following the failure of the Chicago Conference in 1944 to reach a multilateral agreement on the exchange of traffic rights between states, a complex system of many hundreds of bilateral air service agreements has been negotiated which, to a greater or lesser extent, controls routes, capacity and tariffs between the countries concerned. The basic motivation of the agreements has been to safeguard the national aviation interests and even the most liberal of these agreements have been essentially protectionist in pursuing this objective.

It has only recently been recognised by some countries that the protection of national airline interests may be in conflict with the larger economic benefits to be derived from the expansion of tourism. This is one of several factors which are currently leading to new thinking about domestic and international aviation policies. The widespread acceptance of policies of 'economic disengagement' has led many countries to the deregulation of domestic air services, to

the privatisation of previously state-owned airlines and to acceptance of foreign investment in an industry in which 'substantial
ownership and effective control' by nationals has long been a
fundamental proposition.

These changes in government policies are reflected in equally
profound innovations in the structure of the airline industry. The
marketing advantages of large size and developments in communications technology are driving airlines to international alliances
and eventually to cross-border mergers. By the end of this decade
the airline industry will have become a transnational business
dominated by a small number of very large companies with global
networks. These multinational airlines will be free from almost all
forms of economic regulation except those, like competition rules
and merger controls, applying to all industries.

This does not mean that there will be no place in the aviation
industry for smaller airlines but it does mean that their role will
change and that they will operate mainly as 'niche' carriers in
specialised fields. One of the most important areas for niche
marketing will continue to be the development of home territories.
An airline based in one country and having a special interest in the
promotion of traffic to that country will still enjoy the advantage of
special knowledge of its markets. And, particularly in the matter of
developing the tourist traffic of that market, it can identify closely
with the travel industry of the country and remain competitive
against mega-carriers with worldwide concerns. Such airlines may
enjoy the support of their governments because of their commitment
to the development of tourism but they should not need special
protection from foreign competition.

One reason why there have been conflicts between aviation and
tourism policies in some countries is that the benefits of tourism are
not sufficiently well articulated. Tourism objectives need to be
clearly defined so that the benefits can be measured and set against
those of alternative aviation policies. Economic objectives are
usually the most important and include the contribution of tourism
to national income, the creation of employment, net foreign
exchange earnings and government revenues from the taxation of
tourism activities. But, in addition to these economic considerations,
tourism also impacts on social, environmental and cultural aspects
of government policies. A balance sheet of 'potential gains' and
'potential losses' must be drawn up by each country so that the net

benefits of tourism operations can be compared with the net results of aviation policies.

In assessing alternative policies it is essential to have a framework within which the gains and losses can be measured and compared. The problems are different for small countries and large ones, particularly when the smaller countries are less economically developed. A major difference is the degree to which the tourism and airline businesses of each country incur foreign exchange expenditures to provide their services. The import leakages of tourism range from around 40 per cent for small developing countries to well under 10 per cent for highly developed countries. But, even in developing countries, the import leakages of tourism are relatively small compared with those of airline operations. These may be as high as 70 per cent for the airline of a small developing country but they are also likely to be at least 40 per cent for airlines in highly developed countries. This factor is extremely important in judging the foreign exchange merits of alternative policies. Another important factor is the employment created in the aviation and tourism sectors. An equal amount of investment in hotels and aircraft is likely to create almost four times as many jobs in hotels as in airline operations.

Some countries, but by no means all, have paid attention to these considerations in a reassessment of aviation policies which are now seen to have inhibited the growth of tourism. Australia and Mexico have been leaders in this field and both have explicitly recognised that tourism can make a greater economic contribution than protected airlines. Two other countries – Egypt and Thailand – have also adopted a more liberal approach to aviation regulation and have been high in the league table of tourism growth.

It must be acknowledged, however, that many other countries, particularly those in Latin America and Africa, have not yet recognised the benefits of aviation liberalisation and continue to protect their airlines, even though this may be to the detriment of their tourist industries.

A controversial issue in assessing alternative aviation and tourism policies is the role of liberalised regulation of charter services carrying IT holiday packages. Two countries – Turkey and the Dominican Republic – have allowed such services to develop without restraints and have enjoyed exceptional growth rates in the numbers of tourist visitors. Mass market developments of this kind are, however, associated with a relatively low level of average daily spending and large numbers of visitors do not necessarily bring optimal economic benefits and may create other problems. It is for these reasons that some other countries, and the Seychelles and Mauritius are good examples, have banned charter operations in the belief that a lower number of higher-spending visitors on scheduled services produce better net results than a mass market. The Seychelles and Mauritius both also support the proposition that a national airline committed to the development of traffic to its home country is a major benefit for tourism. Both may also find, however, that liberalisation of the regulation of scheduled services is necessary for the tourism growth which they plan.

Many other countries, particularly those where airline and aviation interests have been strongly entrenched, are now debating the significance for them of the worldwide transformation of the air transport industry. Extremely interesting debates are taking place in Kenya, India, Cyprus and South Africa. In each of these countries there is a new recognition of the importance of tourism and each is striving to find an aviation policy which optimises economic and social benefits.

It is not the purpose of this book to make recommendations on the aviation and tourism policies which should be adopted by any particular governments. There are no general answers to the problem of finding the best balance of policies. It is clear from the examination which has been made of policies in many different countries that there are horses for courses: policies which have proved successful in some countries may be inappropriate for others. But there are, nevertheless, some general conclusions which can be drawn from the foregoing studies which have relevance to the worldwide tourism industry.

One such conclusion is that, despite continuing pressure from the World Tourism Organization, the data required for the effective evaluation of alternative aviation and tourism policies are far from complete.

The analysis of the travel and tourism industry of the hypothetical Paradise Island presented in Chapter 4 had the enormous advantage of having made-up data about many aspects of the business which are not so easy to obtain in many real countries. For example, the information about foreign exchange leakages, which is essential for measuring the *net* contribution of each sector, is difficult to obtain and often highly suspect. Similarly, vital information on the average daily expenditure of different kinds of tourist is inadequate in many countries. Moreover, even Paradise Island did not have complete data about such important matters as value added in the tourism sector, the household incomes generated by tourism and government revenues arising directly or indirectly from tourism activities.

It is vitally important that we should know more about the contribution of travel and tourism to national economies. Much more work needs to be undertaken in this field to support the initiative which the WTO has launched with its proposed Standard International Classification of Tourism Activities. It is highly likely that more detailed studies of the value of tourism activities, like those of the World Travel and Tourism Council, will demonstrate the very great economic importance of this industry to almost all countries.

A second general conclusion is that, if the necessary information is collected, it is not difficult for any country to analyse the relative economic benefits of alternative aviation and tourism policies. The framework for such an analysis was established in Chapter 4.

It is readily acknowledged that there are some aspects of both aviation and tourism policies which do not readily lend themselves to a numerical evaluation of costs and benefits. Examples, on the one hand, are the spin-off technological benefits of having a national airline and, on the other hand, the costs of environmental damage from over-rapid tourism expansion. But such costs and benefits are much easier to assess if they can be seen within the framework of the measurable economic results of aviation and tourism activities.

A continuing problem, in striving for the best balance between aviation and tourism policies, is the imbalance between the political 'clout' of the people who represent the interests of the two sectors. It was generally true, in the past, that aviation had a higher level of representation in government than tourism. Moreover, national airlines, particularly when state-owned, were able to exert very strong pressures on government policies. Tourism had a lower status in the political pecking order and the industry, because of its fragmentation, rarely had much influence on policy-making.

In some countries this has now changed and tourism has equal representation with aviation in the government structure, sometimes within a single Ministry of Tourism and Civil Aviation. Where it has occurred, this change is often reflected in a higher priority for tourism in policy formation. Australia is a prime example. But this is not universally true and there are, for example, many instances where inequality is reflected in the titles Director General of Civil

Aviation and Director of Tourism. In yet other countries aviation still has powerful military backing and is administered by the Air Ministry or the Defence Department and air force officers are to be found managing the national airline.

It is therefore recommended that all countries should review the place of aviation and tourism in their governmental structures and ensure that tourism has a status commensurate with the importance of the industry in the national economy. It is further recommended that the tourism business in all countries should ensure that there is an association which is able to speak for the whole industry to governments and the public. Both these recommendations are important to ensure that the tourism sector has an adequate voice in the debates about and the evaluation of the best balance between aviation and tourism policies.

This study has presented case studies of the policies pursued in a sample of countries. Many other countries will recognise their own circumstances in one or more of the examples surveyed. It is to be hoped that they will draw up their own balance sheets of gains and losses from alternative policies and that their economies will benefit from the increase in tourism which radical changes in the world airline industry will make possible in the decade ahead.

Appendix

The case studies

LIBERALISATION SUCCESSES

The first group of case studies concern the policies pursued in four countries – Australia, Mexico, Egypt and Thailand – where tourism has clearly benefited from the adoption of a more liberal approach to the regulation of international air services.

Australia

The new policies adopted in Australia are extremely interesting to this study because they rest on a quite explicit political decision that the potential gains from expanding tourism are greater than the benefits to be derived from protecting a national airline.

Changes in Australian international aviation policy have to be viewed against the background of domestic deregulation which was agreed in 1987 but only became effective in 1990. (This was because three years' notice was required to terminate the agreements by which the previous 'Two Airlines' policy was implemented.) International aviation policy was also influenced by the development of closer links between Australia and New Zealand under the 'Closer Economic Relations' agreement. Both countries are agreed in principle about the desirability of creating a single deregulated air transport market linking them across the Tasman Sea. A further influence was the widespread acceptance of the view that the state-owned Australian and Qantas would benefit from private ownership.

The mood was therefore ready for ending the past restrictive policies in international air service agreements. But the achievement of these policy changes was the result of unprecedented pressures being mounted by the tourism industry with the open support of the Commonwealth Tourism Department.

A concerted campaign, for that is what it was, went on for several years. It was spearheaded by an industry group – the Australian Tourism Industry Association – and the turning point was a *Travel and Tourism Report* by the Industries Assistance Commission in 1989 which recommended a phased programme of aviation regulatory reforms. The Industries Assistance Commission, an independent statutory body advising the government on matters referred to it, came to the following conclusion:

> Regulation of services, government ownership of carriers, and infrastructure and pricing policies impose a high cost on travellers, tourism, the airline industry itself, and the welfare of the Australian people. Fares and costs are higher than they need be, capacity is constrained and even at these prices, Australia is turning away potential customers. Travellers are denied the range of prices and services they would enjoy in a more competitive environment. [p. 59]

The IAC report recommended radical changes in aviation policies, including the privatisation of Australian and Qantas, removing capacity restrictions in bilaterals and allowing foreign investment in domestic airlines.

These and other proposals were vigorously debated in Australia over the following two years and the eventual outcome was that the Labour government adopted even more far-reaching policy changes. These were outlined by the new Prime Minister – Paul Keating – in his 'One Nation' policy statement in February 1992.

The Australian government had already decided in 1991 that it would privatise Australian and Qantas but intended, at that time, to keep the two airlines separate and to apply different criteria for private ownership. Under the new aviation policy the government approved a merger by allowing Qantas to buy-out Australian. The government also announced that 100 per cent of the shares of the merged airline would be sold with the limitations that only 35 per cent of the voting stock could be held by foreign interests and that the government would retain a 'golden share'.

Foreign airlines were invited to apply for a substantial shareholding in Qantas and, in competitive bidding, British Airways beat Singapore Airlines and, in December 1992, acquired 25 per cent of the equity and three seats of the twelve-member board of directors. Through this investment in Qantas, British Airways also acquired a link with Air New Zealand because Qantas already had a 20 per cent stake in that airline.

In parallel with these changes in the structure of Australian airline industry, radical changes were also announced in national aviation policy. Shortly after the Prime Minister's 'One Nation' statement the Minister of Shipping and Aviation published details of the new aviation policy in a document entitled *Australian Aviation: Towards the 21st Century*. The tourism implications of the policy were enlarged upon in a subsequent publication from the Commonwealth Minister of Tourism called *Tourism: Australia's Passport to Growth*. The key elements are:

- The abandonment of the previous policy of designating only Qantas for international routes and the introduction of a multi-designation policy to introduce more competition.
- To negotiate more liberal and flexible air service agreements in which tourism interests are taken fully into account.
- To ensure that charter policy gives adequate recognition to the needs of the tourism industry.

It remains to be seen what the outcome of the new aviation policy will be. It is entirely clear, however, that Australia is giving a very high priority to the development of tourism. It has established a separate Ministry of Tourism and given it Cabinet status. Tourism, as shown in Figure 9, is already Australia's biggest export business and, in the Ministry of Tourism's high-growth scenario, the number of tourist visitors is targeted to grow from 2.4 million in 1991 to 6.5 million in 2000.

Mexico

International tourism is very big business in Mexico. Arrivals increased from 4.6 million in 1986 to 6.4 million in 1990: an increase of 39 per cent, compared with the world average of 34 per cent. Over 90 per cent of Mexico's tourist visitors come from the United States and almost 70 per cent come by air. It is obvious that by far the most important issue in Mexican international aviation policy is the bilateral relationship with the United States.

This relationship has been influenced by domestic aviation developments in Mexico. Like Australia, Mexico has deregulated its domestic air services. It did so in 1991. It has also pursued a privatisation programme as a result of which Aeromexico (which was declared bankrupt in 1988) is now entirely privately owned and Mexicana only has a 32 per cent government shareholding. It has been reported that Aeromexico may take over the financially troubled Mexicana. Aeromexico spread its wings at the end of 1992 and acquired a 70 per cent shareholding in AeroPeru, the formerly state-owned national airline of Peru. On the domestic front, a new privately owned airline – TAESA – has entered the scene and it won a 10 per cent share of domestic traffic in 1992.

There is, of course, a huge disparity between the size and wealth of Mexico and those of the United States. It is not surprising that Mexico has acted warily in its past air transport relationship with its rich and powerful neighbour. For many years the entry of foreign airlines to Mexico was restricted to Mexico City and all air transport to other destinations was by domestic air services. All that has changed and there are now direct international air services to seven Mexican destinations in addition to Mexico City. Cancun, an entirely new resort created barely twenty years ago, had well over 2 million air passenger arrivals in 1990 and is served by ten foreign and two Mexican airlines.

The bilateral relationship between Mexico and the United States developed slowly. Until the mid-1980s the limited capacities of Mexican airlines inhibited liberalisation. The 1988 agreement between the two countries was a landmark in aviation policy. It undoubtedly resulted from a revised Mexican view about the economic importance of tourism and the desirability of increasing the numbers of US tourist visitors.

The most important liberalising aspect of the 1988 bilateral agreement was the increased scope it gave for multiple designation of airlines. Before 1988 this was allowed but not on the same route. The 1988 agreement allowed the splitting of routes and the designation of different airlines for each of them. For example, a previous route New York–Houston–Mexico City could be split as two routes – New York–Mexico City and Houston–Mexico City – and each could have its own designated airline.

The 1991 US–Mexico bilateral was a further major step in liberalisation. Services can now be operated between any international airports in the two countries. There is only one route in the agreement and that is all points in the United States and all points in Mexico. These are, of course, limited to airports with adequate facilities for international services but there is an agreed list of such airports in each country. The general rule is that only one airline from each country will operate each city-pair but about forty routes have been specified on which two airlines from each country are allowed to operate.

It is likely that further liberalisation will follow and that a future agreement will eliminate the remaining restrictions on operations so that there will be multiple designation on all routes.

Figure 10 shows the growth of air traffic between the US and Mexico from 1986 to 1991. It shows that the Mexican airlines have been quite successful in maintaining their market position despite the increased competitive opportunities which the liberalised bilateral has given US airlines.

Figure 10 also shows that charter operations have played a relatively small role in the US–Mexico market, being only 12 per cent of the total in 1991. It must be noted, however, that charter services have an above-average importance in traffic to Cancun. Airport statistics show that about 25 per cent of Cancun air arrivals in 1990 were on non-scheduled services.

Mexico's experience indicates that liberalised aviation regulation can be a great benefit to tourism without harming the operations of the national airlines of the receiving country.

Egypt

Tourist visitors to Egypt increased by 94 per cent from 1.24 million in 1986 to 2.41 million in 1990. About two-thirds of all visitors arrive by air but if travel from neighbouring countries, like Libya and Sudan, is excluded the air share is over 80 per cent. The rapid growth in Egypt's tourist traffic has been associated with significant relaxations in the regulation of air services and the Egyptian experience must be regarded as one of the successes of liberalisation even though doubts remain about some restrictions in the aviation policies pursued.

There is no doubt that the government of Egypt fully recognises the vital importance of tourism in its national economy. Gross foreign exchange receipts from tourism in 1990 were $1.99 billion and the industry employed over 60,000 people.

Following a general liberalisation of economic policies in the mid-1970s, there was a gradual easing of aviation regulation. Some competition was encouraged on domestic routes because it was thought that the national airline – Egyptair – was damaging tourism by the poor performance and inadequate capacity on routes between Cairo, Luxor and Aswan.

Tourism pressures, competition and better management in the 1980s greatly improved Egyptair's performance and the airline embarked on a major development programme to update its fleet and through its travel subsidiary – Karnak – to enhance its market position. The strengthened status of the national airline enabled the government to adopt more liberal policies in the international field and it invited private airlines to introduce scheduled services on routes not served by Egyptair. Despite this, competitive services have been slow to develop and, as shown in Figure 11, Egyptair has increased its share of scheduled international traffic.

Liberalisation has also been extended to charter operations and, although these have effectively been excluded from Cairo, they have now become quite important to other destinations. Nevertheless, as also shown in Figure 11, charter traffic is still a relatively small percentage of total traffic.

The core of Egyptian tourism is based on the antiquities of the Nile Valley. The government is, however, very interested in diversification and has been encouraging the development of beach traffic to new resorts on the Red Sea and in the Gulf of Aqaba. Liberalised air services, particularly charters to Hurghada and Sharm-el-Sheik, are playing an important role in the success of these new developments.

Thailand

There are interesting similarities between developments in Thailand and in Egypt. Tourist visitors to Thailand increased by 88 per cent from 2.82 million in 1986 to 5.3 million in 1990. Air traffic was over 80 per cent of total visitors and the remarkable growth of tourism was clearly related to a relaxation of aviation regulation.

Gross foreign exchange earnings from tourism in 1990 were $4.3 billion and the industry was Thailand's largest earner of foreign exchange. Over 30 per cent of visitors came from Europe but the biggest market was the Asia/Pacific area, which accounted for more than half of all traffic. About 90 per cent of all visitors said that 'leisure' was the primary reason for their visit.

An 'open skies' aviation policy was adopted in 1989 and this resulted in a large increase in international services. The number of airlines serving Bangkok increased from forty-nine in 1989 to sixty-two in 1990 and to sixty-seven in 1991. But despite this liberalisation of international regulation, the national airline – Thai International – has, as shown in Figure 12, retained a substantial share of the traffic.

The liberalisation of charter regulation has had surprisingly little effect, largely because the scheduled airlines have offered tour operators competitive seat prices. Less than 5 per cent of air visitors arrive on charter flights and these are mainly operated to secondary destinations like Phuket. Restrictions are likely to increase on charter operations at Bangkok because of capacity constraints and the result will probably be an increase of charters to other resorts like Chiang Mai and Pattaya.

Thailand has become an expensive country to visit: prices are generally about 20 per cent higher than in Singapore. But this has clearly not deterred the growth of tourism and the country continues to enjoy a daily average spending level of $115 for each tourist visitor. Visitors from some Asian countries, like Japan, Taiwan and Korea, spend much more per day than this average: for Japan the figure is as high as $146.

Thailand has given some encouragement to new airlines to compete with Thai International and new services have been introduced on both domestic and international routes. Bangkok Airways has taken over part of Thai International's domestic network and two other new airlines – Tropical Sea Air and SKAir – have started domestic services. Bangkok Airways has also recently started limited international services on regional routes in South East Asia.

It would be wrong, in the cases of both Thailand and Egypt, to attribute all their success in the remarkable development of tourism to the relaxation of aviation regulation. Neither country has yet adopted a complete liberalisation of its international regime: both still rely heavily on bilateral bargaining. Nevertheless their achievements in the tourism field must be counted as successes for more liberal aviation policies.

LINGERING PROTECTIONISM

Most countries recognise the force of changes in the world airline industry described in Chapter 3 and at least pay lip service to the proposition that their tourist industries may benefit from the adoption of more liberal aviation policies. There are, however, some exceptions.

Brazil

One of the most interesting exceptions is Brazil, which has recently set out its reasons for continuing a protectionist international aviation policy. The Brazilian Department of Civil Aviation published a White Paper called *Commercial Air Transport Service Policy* in March 1992. It was based on the conclusions reached at a National Commercial Aviation Conference at which all segments of the air transport industry were represented, and the policy was officially approved by the Air Minister.

The new policy is concerned with domestic as well as international air transport policy but it is the latter which is more significant for the purposes of this study. The basic elements of the international aviation policy adopted by the Brazilian government are as follows:

- To maintain the principles of bilateral negotiation and agreements, avoiding opposing multilateral air transport agreements, in defence of Brazilian interests.
- To pursue policies designed to protect the Brazilian civil aviation market.
- To maintain the principle of predetermining capacity.
- To maintain control of tariffs by requiring double approval.
- To require renegotiation of traffic rights if the ownership of a foreign airline ceases to belong to nationals of the country concerned.

These protectionist policies are at variance with the avowed freer trade objectives of the Mercosur agreement in which Brazil is a participant with Argentina, Paraguay and Uruguay. The air transport White Paper acknowledges this problem but says bluntly that, because the Brazilian air transport market is more than half the total for the continent, and there will not be 'any corresponding counter- advantage', it will not adopt policies which are not compatible with the commercial interests and objectives of Brazilian airlines.

It is significant that the White Paper makes not a single mention of the interests of the tourism industry. This appears to reflect the low priority attached to the development of tourism and the remarkable decline in the number of tourist visitors over the past several years. The number of international tourist visitors fell by 44 per cent from 1.9 million in 1986 to 1.1 million in 1990. Tourism earnings are now less than 5 per cent of total export earnings and hotels are predominantly occupied by domestic clients.

Two developments might change the Brazilian situation. The first might be the emergence of a stronger voice to speak for the interests of the tourism industry. The second might be a reorganisation which gave commercial aviation an independent *civil* role in government, removing it from the Air Ministry. The effect of this might be to reduce the dominant position of the airlines in the formulation of aviation policies and to strengthen the position of other interests, particularly those of the tourist industry.

Other Latin American countries

Five other Latin American countries – Bolivia, Colombia, Ecuador, Peru and Venezuela – have joined together in the Andean Pact to liberalise trade within this area. The Andean Pact theoretically established an 'open skies' aviation policy between its five members but it has become apparent that the signatories were not willing to accept a deregulated air transport regime. Only Colombia and Venezuela, by a bilateral agreement, have made any progress towards air transport liberalisation. These are the two members of the Andean Pact with the largest numbers of international tourist visitors.

Developing countries in Africa

Many developing countries in Africa continue to pursue restrictive aviation policies designed to protect their national airlines. There are some special cases, and specific commentaries are included later on the policies of Kenya, the Seychelles and Mauritius, each of which offers particular lessons in studying the relationships between aviation and tourism policies. And there are other exceptions, like Gambia, which has built up a substantial tourist traffic (101,000 visitors in 1990) by encouraging the IT traffic of foreign operators without regard to the protection of scheduled services.

For the most part, however, aviation policies in Africa have endeavoured to protect the scheduled services of the national airline and put limits on the operations of foreign airlines. The arguments used to justify these policies are that:

- The country must have its own airline for the national policy reasons discussed in Chapter 3.
- That the national airline would not survive if it had to face unrestricted competition with much larger and stronger foreign airlines.
- A national airline adds to the pride and independence of the country.
- Protection is necessary until such time as African airlines can be strengthened, through co-operation, to meet foreign competition.

It is often said that the basic problem for African airlines is how to cope with the radical changes which are occurring in the world aviation industry. In what they hope will be a transitional period, many African countries cling to the features of the bilateral system which, through the principle of fair and equal opportunity, gives them opportunities to obtain economic benefits by bargaining traffic rights.

The developing countries of Africa recognise that their small (and often inefficient) airlines will not be able to survive independently. Collaboration is seen to be essential but action in this field is painfully slow. The much-lauded Yamoussoukro Declaration, signed by African Ministers in 1988, set out 'A new African air transport policy' with a programme for co-operation in many areas of airline operations. A more recent meeting of 'A Workshop on Air Transport in Africa' in Addis Ababa in 1992 once again catalogued the problems of small African airlines and repeated proposals for co-operation and joint action. But almost nothing has been done to implement these and other resolutions.

And, while these proposals for airline co-operation continue to be debated, most of the countries involved maintain restrictions on the operations of foreign airlines. There can be little doubt that, in many cases, these capacity restrictions are detrimental to the development of tourism.

CHARTER BOOMS

Two countries with high rates of growth of international visitors are shown in Figure 8 to be Turkey and the Dominican Republic. Visitors to Turkey increased by 131 per cent from 1986 to 1990 and visitors to the Dominican Republic increased by 75 per cent over the same period. Both countries achieved these high growth rates by allowing unfettered charter operations and encouraging low-price inclusive tour packages.

The Turkish boom

About 89 per cent of all visitors to Turkey in 1990 were tourists and, as shown in Figure 13, this segment of inbound travel grew by 131 per cent from 1986 to 1990.

About 36 per cent of total visitors in 1990 arrived by road but the largest transport sector was air, which accounted for 48 per cent of visitors. Figure 14 shows that air arrivals from 1986 to 1990 grew even faster than total arrivals and air increased its share of total traffic over the period. This very large increase in air traffic was mainly caused by the liberalisation of Turkish policy regulating charter operations with the resulting increase in charter traffic shown in Figure 15. Tour operators and their associated charter airlines in Western Europe, particularly in the United Kingdom and Germany, were looking for new opportunities to expand their markets and promote destinations rather further afield than Spain, and they seized the chance to open up the Turkish holiday market. The 49 per cent increase in Turkish air arrivals in 1988 reflected a spectacular doubling of air traffic from the United Kingdom. Charter traffic, which was equal to scheduled traffic in 1986, was almost double scheduled by 1990.

Turkey's foreign exchange earnings have increased in line with its growing tourist traffic. Figures for earlier years are somewhat suspect because of widespread concealment, but earnings are now well over $3 billion a year and are at least 20 per cent of the value of Turkish exports.

No official information is available on the average daily expenditure of tourists in Turkey but it is estimated to be about $75. This is consistent with figures for other countries which have a high percentage of IT charter traffic. Turkish tourism would clearly benefit from an increase in higher-rated traffic but, in general, the charter boom has produced considerable economic benefits.

The boom in the Dominican Republic

Visitors to the Dominican Republic increased to over 1.5 million in 1990, which made this market roughly equal to the Bahamas and surpassed in the Caribbean only by Puerto Rico in the number of visitors.

Virtually all tourists to the Dominican Republic arrive by air and the growth of tourist traffic reflects the 'open skies' policy which has been adopted by the government.

The Dominican Republic is served by scheduled services from four cities in the United States. From Europe, scheduled services are operated by Air France, Lufthansa and Iberia. It is, however, the growth of IT charter services from Europe, including the United Kingdom, and Canada which has had a major impact on the growth of tourism to the Dominican Republic.

It is estimated that tourism now contributes over 10 per cent to the GNP of the Dominican Republic and the growth of this industry has been of vital economic importance as the sugar industry has declined. Tourism is the biggest earner of foreign exchange: tourism earnings are equal to half of total export earnings.

Tourism has also become vitally important in employment. It has been estimated that over 40,000 people were directly employed in tourism in 1990 and that the same number of people also owed their jobs indirectly to activities created by tourism.

The Dominican Republic offers many attractions to tourists, not least its climate, beaches and mountains. But the primary reason for its great success in increasing visitor traffic is that it is the cheapest destination in the Caribbean. Good hotel rooms are available at $30 per day and other prices are low. The consequence of this, however, is that the average expenditures of tourist visitors are less than $60 per day. There has, in fact, been a decline in the average spending of tourists as the traffic volume has increased and this reflects the increasing proportion of visitors arriving on low-price IT charters. The vast majority of visitors from Europe now come on packaged tours.

Like Turkey, where the charter boom has been based on large numbers of low-spending visitors, the tourist industry of the Dominican Republic would benefit from an increase in higher-spending clients. But this is difficult to achieve once a low-cost ethos has been established. An *Economist* Intelligence Unit report commented on the problem and concluded: 'The heavy growth orientation of the sector has encouraged an attitude among many in the industry to emphasize quantity instead of quality.'

Such attitudes are difficult to change and an environment of this kind makes it hard to produce the standards of personal service expected by more affluent visitors.

CHARTER BANS

Two countries – the Seychelles and Mauritius – have concluded that their tourism industries are best served by a ban on charter operations.

Policies in the Seychelles

Tourist visitors to the Seychelles grew from 67,000 in 1986 to 104,000 in 1990. This increase of 55 per cent, though not as spectacular as the booms in Turkey and the Dominican Republic, was well above the world average growth of tourist arrivals in the same period.

Virtually all tourist visitors come by air and, moreover, almost all come on scheduled services. The Seychelles is well served by scheduled services: five airlines, including Air Seychelles, currently operate from ten overseas points with a total of twenty-four weekly services.

The Seychelles has pursued a restrictive policy on charters. The government has decreed that 'charter operations will be permitted when they do not adversely affect the viability of scheduled services' and, in practice, this has meant an almost total ban on charters. The official reason is that past experience has taught the Seychelles not to allow its tourism industry to rely on airlines which lack long-term commitment to the island. The perceived lack of commitment is seen as a strong reason to discourage charters. Another reason is the belief that charters attract a less discriminating, low-spending clientele which would conflict with the national tourism policy of controlling growth to protect the social and natural environment.

The practical effect of these policies has been that only three series of charter flights have been operated to the Seychelles, each tightly regulated. An Italian company – Air Europe – was given temporary rights to operate in lieu of Alitalia as a quasi-scheduled service; Lufthansa's subsidiary Condor was permitted to operate in lieu of Lufthansa; and a South African airline was given temporary permission to operate pending the designation of a scheduled airline. The experiences of all three of these operations confirmed the opinion of the Seychelles authorities that charter flights were undesirable: that they were inherently unreliable and led to the promotion of lower-spending traffic.

The Seychelles statement on aviation and tourism policies says that the government will adopt 'a liberal but well monitored approach' in the granting of international traffic rights and will encourage foreign airlines to expand their services to Mahe, the largest of the islands. The government supports the operations of the national airline – Air Seychelles – but declares that its objective is not to protect the national airline but to promote the tourism industry by ensuring that reliable and diverse air links are provided.

Gross foreign exchange earnings from tourism in 1990 were $120 million and reflect an unusually high average expenditure level of $115 per day. It is not easy to say how far this high level of spending (almost double that for the Dominican Republic) is a result of the virtual ban on charter operations but it is certainly the view of hoteliers and travel agents in the Seychelles that the government's aviation policy has been successful in keeping out low-spending tourists on low-price packaged tours. Based on Seychelles experience, it does appear that the tour operators who use scheduled services do develop and promote a higher-quality and higher-priced product than those associated exclusively with charter operations.

Foreign exchange earnings from tourism, as noted in Chapter 4, can be substantially diluted by the leakage of expenditures on imports to meet visitor needs. In the case of the Seychelles it has been estimated in Chapter 4 that the direct leakage (excluding the 'induced' imports expenditures) is about 30 per cent of gross foreign exchange earnings.

There can be little doubt that this level of leakage is very much lower than that for Air Seychelles, which, with expatriate crews and foreign aircraft maintenance, probably spends at least 70 per cent of its total costs in foreign currencies. (The Air Seychelles annual report for 1991 gives an even higher figure. It says that foreign exchange receipts were SR175 million and foreign currency payments were SR170 million.)

The model of Paradise Island presented in Chapter 4 is therefore highly relevant to the Seychelles. If the protection of Air Seychelles restricted the growth of tourism it would be highly likely that this would have adverse effects on net foreign exchange earnings and employment.

It may be, however, that the tourism policy adopted by the Seychelles effectively takes these potential losses into account. The Seychelles has made it clear that it does not want to develop a mass tourism market. It has concluded that, for social and environmental reasons, it should limit the number of tourist visitors. The present policy suggests limiting the number of tourists staying in licensed accommodation in the three main islands, Mahe, Praslin and La Digne, to 4,000 at any one time. This implies a target of no more than 150,000 annual visitors, unless the smaller islands are substantially developed. Present policy also proposes that all new hotels shall be at least international four-star standard and that establishments of 100 rooms or less will be encouraged.

A debate is now taking place in the Seychelles about the validity of these limits and, in some quarters, it is being suggested that an upper limit of half a million visitors a year would be economically sensible and environmentally sustainable. If such a change were adopted it would make a review of aviation policy necessary.

Aviation problems may arise if foreign airlines, in the new global scenario described in Chapter 3, press for reduced fares and offer standards of service and marketing which Air Seychelles cannot match. In such circumstances the Seychelles reconsideration of aviation policy may force Air Seychelles to seek an alliance with a major foreign airline to survive.

Mauritius policies

In some respects the aviation and tourism policies of Mauritius are similar to those of the Seychelles, particularly in the ban on charters and the pursuit of high-spending visitor traffic. But Mauritius has a much larger tourism industry and much more ambitious plans for future growth.

Visitor traffic grew from 165,000 in 1986 to 292,000 in 1990. This 77 per cent increase put Mauritius high in the world league of growth countries. (See Figure 8.)

Virtually all visitors came by air and all on scheduled services. The ban on charter services is designed to protect the markets of scheduled airlines, particularly the national airline – Air Mauritius – which carries over 55 per cent of total passenger traffic.

Mauritius is well served by an excellent network of scheduled services linking it with the major markets of Europe, South Africa, East Africa and South East Asia: it is served by eleven international airlines which operate direct services to twenty-two destinations. Price competition between the airlines is limited and, because Mauritius is a very long way from its major markets, fares are high and tend to be a high percentage, perhaps over 60 per cent, of the total cost of a holiday.

Tourism is economically important to Mauritius. It is estimated that over 46,000 people are directly or indirectly employed in the industry: about 10 per cent of the total working population. Tourism contributed over 10 per cent to GDP.

Foreign exchange earnings in 1990 were $264 million but some estimates have assessed the leakage of expenditure on imports as high as 90 per cent. Excluding the 'induced' imports, a more realistic figure is 43 per cent, but, even so, the leakage is high and calls for increasing attention to be paid to ways of increasing the local inputs.

Tourism in Mauritius faces two major problems. First, like many other countries, there is the threat of environmental damage arising from over-rapid expansion. Second is the threat of serious over-capacity in accommodation facilities. Some new controls have been introduced but there are still plans for a massive increase in the number of hotel rooms in the next few years. Moreover, there are no controls on the boom in self-catering holiday accommodation, which continues unabated. The pressures of over-capacity in the accommodation sector seem certain to lead to calls for an easing of restrictions in aviation policy. Some hoteliers are already trying to persuade the government to allow charter flights in off-season months. And there will be pressure for lower fares on scheduled services and for increases in the frequencies allowed for foreign airlines.

The dilemma for the government of Mauritius is that it wants to retain the 'high-quality' image of the island as a tourist destination, and the high average level of spending of its visitors, but it has allowed capacity to run ahead of that type of demand. Something has to be changed. It remains to be seen whether aviation policies will be liberalised to encourage a greater number of visitors or whether effective planning controls will be introduced to match accommodation capacity to the demands of high-spending visitors.

SOME EVOLVING POLICIES

It is not surprising, in the light of the complexities of the issues already discussed, that many countries have found it difficult to find the right balance between their aviation and tourism policies. Moreover, the decisions have often been made even more difficult by differences in the relative political influence of the people who represent the interests of the two major segments of the travel and tourism industry. In many countries the airline industry is more unified and more strongly represented than tourism in policy debates. It often happens that the tourism industry is fragmented, does not speak with an agreed voice, and does not have the same level of representation in government as aviation. In such circumstances there are likely to be equivocations and contradictions in the aviation and tourism policies pursued. But, in many countries, these uncertainties are also accompanied by a vigorous debate about how best to react to the drastic changes which are transforming the world airline industry. This section focuses on the current debates in four countries – Kenya, India, Cyprus and South Africa – which throw light on the problems of arriving at an optimal balance between the interests of aviation and tourism.

Kenya

Kenya is an excellent example of a country struggling to find the most appropriate balance between aviation and tourism policies. Tourist visitors grew by 35 per cent from 604,000 in 1986 to 814,000 in 1990. This was only just above the world average and new efforts are being made to expand the market, both for Kenya alone and in co-operation with other countries to promote multi-country packages.

Tourism is important in Kenya's economy. It employs over 110,000 people and earned $443 million in foreign exchange in 1990. These gross receipts from tourism were equal to over 40 per cent of earnings from the export of commodities.

The national airline – Kenya Airways – enjoys a high degree of protection on scheduled services but a lot of new competition has been authorised in the charter field. The regulation of scheduled services remains essentially 'predeterministic'. All bilateral agreements and their related 'confidential memoranda of understanding' specify:

- Single designation.
- Agreement on the capacity and frequency of services to be operated by each airline.
- Equal division of capacity between Kenya Airways and the designated foreign airline.
- The approval of fares by both governments.

Some memoranda also specify that a royalty payment shall be made to Kenya Airways when the foreign airline operates more capacity than Kenya Airways.

These protectionist policies to regulate scheduled services are in marked contrast with the policies which have been adopted in recent years to allow the operation of charter services. With the proviso that they operate to Mombasa, and not to Nairobi, licences for charter operations have been issued on a fairly liberal basis. Kenya Airways has protested to the Civil Aviation Board that charter operations are adversely affecting the financial results of scheduled services but these objections have largely been overruled and charter licences granted on the grounds that they are 'in the public interest'.

As a result of these policies there were three Kenyan airlines and sixteen European charter companies operating charter services in summer 1992. Together they operated more than thirty flights between Europe and Mombasa each week. The effects on scheduled operations are illustrated in Figure 16. Kenya Airways' scheduled traffic remained static while that of foreign scheduled services declined. Kenya Airways introduced some charter flights of its own but the traffic on them was small and the only real growth was that of foreign charters.

Holiday traffic is the predominant category of travel to Kenya. In the past the holiday visitors came primarily on safari to visit Kenya's extensive game reserves. A new type of traffic has been created by charter operations, and beach holidays on the Indian Ocean coast have been promoted by inclusive tour operators, particularly from Germany and the United Kingdom. Many visitors to Kenya combine a game park safari with a beach holiday and this makes a very attractive package. But there has also been a substantial growth in 'beach only' holiday traffic, much of it at low prices.

The contribution of 'beach only' traffic to the economy of Kenya is undoubtedly much lower than that of safari traffic. A World Bank report concluded that the inclusion of a wildlife component in a packaged tour ensures not only greater earnings but also that a higher percentage of earnings are retained within the country than is the case with beach holidays. Moreover, as well as contributing more to the economy, safari traffic is a more stable long-term basis for developing Kenya's tourist traffic. The country's wild-life attractions are almost unique whereas the beaches compete in the European market with equally attractive resorts in many other parts of the world.

It seems probable, in the foreseeable future, that the government of Kenya will want to retain and protect its national airline. It has, however, become interested in the privatisation of Kenya Airways and would almost certainly welcome a foreign partner in such a venture. This might lead to a liberalisation of the regulation of scheduled services whilst at the same time introducing more regulation in the charter field. There is a good case for requiring the promoters of IT charter services to demonstrate that their operations make a significant contribution to Kenya's economy. Other countries have adopted such policies and have, for example, made it a condition of a charter licence that IT visitors should spend a specified minimum in the country.

It remains to be seen what will emerge from Kenya's review of aviation and tourism policies. Much will depend on the current efforts which are being made to increase the efficiency and profitability of Kenya Airways and its success in negotiating a strategic alliance. Both Kenya Airways and Kenya tourist companies suffer from being 'at the wrong end of the route' and much has to be done to overcome these marketing disadvantages.

India

The growth of tourist arrivals in India has been slow: visits increased by only 18 per cent from 1.45 million in 1986 to 1.71 million in 1990. The traffic volume is quite large but, relative to India's size, international tourist traffic is small. It has, indeed, been compared unfavourably with that of Singapore and Hong Kong, which both attracted more than 5 million tourist visitors. Nevertheless, India's earnings from tourism are important to its economy and contributed $1.4 billion in gross foreign exchange earnings in 1990.

Aviation policy is equivocal. A new policy introduced as part of an economic liberalisation packaged by Prime Minister Narasimha Rao in 1991 was described as 'open skies'. It is far from being that. The government has promised to deregulate domestic operations and has said that it will repeal the Air Corporations Act of 1953 which gives monopoly rights to the two state-owned airlines – Air India for international traffic and Indian Airlines for domestic services and a limited number of regional routes. New entrants are being allowed to operate on domestic routes on non-scheduled licences but, so far, only one new airline has been able to take advantage of these new opportunities.

In the international field, scheduled services are still closely regulated and Air India retains its status as the primary Indian international airline. Air India strongly resists the pressures from foreign airlines, particularly US airlines, wishing to increase their routes and the capacity of their services.

The 1991 aviation policy liberalised the operations of charter services to India. Previously charters had been allowed only to minor destinations, like Goa, but since 1991 they can be authorised to the major cities. The system for licensing charter flights has been simplified but important new qualifications have been introduced. The most important new rule is that charter operators have to guarantee that each IT passenger will spend a specified minimum amount in India. The amount specified is $350 for a seven-day visit in the period 1 October to 31 March and $300 in the period from 1 April to 30 September. All tourists have to be booked for their packaged tours in the originating country and their stay in India has to be a minimum of seven days and a maximum of forty-five days. In addition there is an explicit ban on 'seat only' sales.

These limitations on charter operations have two effects. The first is to ensure that charters bring a minimum level of tourist spending into India and do not unduly dilute the average daily spend. The second is to protect Air India scheduled services from the loss of ethnic traffic. Large numbers of Indians resident overseas return to India for a holiday, family or business visit. Not many spend as much as $50 per day in India and are thus precluded from using charter flights. Nevertheless, charter operations may play an important new role in developing tourist traffic to India.

The view of Air India management is that they would welcome a more competitive international aviation regime if they were freed from governmental restrictions, particularly limitations on investment in new aircraft. The government has agreed, in principle, that both state-owned airlines should be privatised but proposes to retain a 51 per cent shareholding in Air India. Moreover, foreign investments will be limited to less than 10 per cent. Experience from other countries suggests that such limitations on privatisation defeat the objective of freeing the airline from governmental control and inhibit private investment.

The then Minister of Tourism and Civil Aviation, Madhavrao Scindia, declared in 1992 that the government is committed to the liberalisation of international air services and said that 'incoming capacity will not be pegged with the growth of Air India'. But he went on to say:

> In the process of liberalisation we cannot kill the commercial interests of our own national carrier. In no country is this done. We have to keep our commercial interests in mind. Agreements are reciprocal in nature and there is always give and take. There must be something in return for what we give.

It is clear that liberalisation in India is a far cry from 'open skies'. What the government seems to have in mind is the encouragement of new services from countries not adequately covered. The Minister spoke of the considerable potential for tourism development out of Scandinavia and Korea. He hoped for a more liberal framework of operations with the airlines of those countries.

The policy debate in India continues. It may well be influenced by new moves for the tourist industry to get together to formulate policy proposals and to act as a lobby in support of liberalisation measures which it believes to be in the best interests of tourism development.

Cyprus

Cyprus has enjoyed a high rate of growth of tourist visitors, with an 89 per cent increase from 828,000 in 1986 to 1.56 million in 1990. In 1990 87 per cent of these visitors came by air. The economic importance of tourism is reflected in the $1.26 billion gross foreign exchange earnings in 1990.

A major factor in the growth of tourist traffic to Cyprus has been the rapid development of IT charter operations from Western Europe, particularly the United Kingdom. Figure 17 shows that traffic on IT charter services grew threefold from 1986 to 1990 and by 1990 such services carried over 40 per cent of all air arrivals.

Cyprus might well have been included in Chapter 5 as a charter boom country but there have been doubts about the consequences of this aspect of aviation policy, as explained later.

Its charter operations until 1991 were almost entirely undertaken by foreign airlines. The national airline – Cyprus Airways – retained more than half the scheduled traffic but saw that this market was stagnating as charters increased. A policy review in 1991 led to the establishment of a new charter airline – Eurocypria – as a subsidiary of Cyprus Airways. Eurocypria has its own management team but leases its aircraft from Cyprus Airways. Although the initial operations of Eurocypria in 1992 are reported to have been successful, they involve only two aircraft, and the relatively small scale of these operations is unlikely to make a major impact on the distribution of traffic, with foreign airlines still carrying the major share.

Cyprus-based airlines and tour operators have great difficulty in competing for traffic in the major originating markets. The extensive advertising and other marketing activities of the companies based in the traffic-originating countries are powerful advantages. They create strong preferences for their own services and foreign companies from the destination countries find it difficult to compete.

Cyprus has tried to overcome these problems by setting up its own tour-promoting company in the United Kingdom, the market which produces almost half its foreign visitors. A new company – Cyprair Tours Ltd – was established in 1991 as a specialist tour operator organising IT packages from several UK cities and having the flexibility to offer travel either on Eurocypria or Cyprus Airways scheduled services.

Like other markets which are predominantly served by IT charter operations, the average level of tourist spending in Cyprus is relatively low: it is estimated at about $80 per day in 1990. The greatest difficulty in increasing the level of earnings in a tourist economy dominated by IT operations is the enormous bargaining strength of large-scale tour companies which are able to negotiate very low rates for hotel rooms.

Hoteliers and other segments of the tourist industry in Cyprus are now concerned about the country's aviation policies. Further moves to liberalise the regulation of scheduled operations, and the authorisation of more services by foreign airlines, are seen as leading to a further weakening of the position of Cyprus Airways. There are fears in the tourism industry that if all air services, scheduled and charter, are dominated by foreign airlines and foreign tour companies, the results will be further reductions in room rates and tourist spending levels.

It is for this reason that aviation and tourism policies are issues currently being debated in Cyprus and why the country is included in this chapter on evolving policies.

South Africa

Tourist visitors to South Africa increased by 60 per cent from 645,000 in 1986 to 1.03 million in 1990. Only 52 per cent of these visitors in 1990 came by air: 46 per cent came by road from other African countries. These other African countries accounted for over half of all visitors to South Africa, compared with Europe's share of 34 per cent.

Radical political changes and the ending of sanctions are transforming the prospects for tourism to South Africa. The government recognises these opportunities and has moved towards more liberal aviation policies.

Domestic operations have been deregulated and new airlines are now operating in competition with South African Airways. In the international field, the new importance attached to the development of tourism has led the government to declare that its future negotiation of bilateral agreements will provide for multi-designation of airlines, the elimination of capacity restrictions and the abolition of tariff controls.

South Africa intends, however, to maintain rather restrictive control of charter operations. Charters will be limited to a maximum of 400 flights a year or no more than 10 per cent of the number of scheduled flights. The Tourism Minister, Org Marais, has said: 'It is imperative to stress that South Africa does not wish to become a cheap charter area but wishes to promote itself as a quality destination.' It remains to seen what impact these policies will have on the development of tourism in South Africa, particularly whether the charter policy will achieve the objective of a high average level of daily spending by tourist visitors.

Bibliography

Annual reports of airlines and of national tourist organisations.

Archer, Brian (1977) *Tourism in the Bahamas and Bermuda*, Cardiff: University of Wales Press.

Archer, Brian (1981) *The Economic Impact of Tourism in Mauritius*, Washington, D.C.: World Bank.

Archer, Brian (1982) *The Economic Impact of Tourism in the Seychelles*, London: Commonwealth Secretariat.

Australia, Government of (1989) *Report on Travel and Tourism*, Canberra: Industries Assistance Commission.

Australia, Government of (1992) *Australian Aviation: Towards the Twenty-first Century*, Canberra: Commonwealth Department of Shipping and Aviation.

Australia, Government of (1992) *Tourism: Australia's Passport to Growth*, Canberra: Commonwealth Department of Tourism.

Boeing Aircraft Company (1993) *Current Marketing Outlook: World Market Demand and Airplane Supply Requirements*, Seattle: Boeing.

Brazil, Government of (1992) *Civil Aviation: Brazilian Commercial Air Transport Service Policy*, Brasilia: Department of Civil Aviation.

Button, Kenneth, and Swann, Dennis (1989) *The Age of Regulatory Reform*, Oxford: Clarendon Press.

Cheng, Bin (1962) *The Law of International Air Transport*, London: Stevens.

Cleverdon, Richard (1979) *The Economic and Social Impact of International Tourism on Developing Countries*, London: *Economist* Intelligence Unit.

Doganis, Rigas (1991) *Flying off Course: The Economics of International Airlines*, London: HarperCollins.

Economist Intelligence Unit (1990) *Dominican Republic*, International Tourism Reports, No. 1, London: *Economist* Intelligence Unit.

Economist Intelligence Unit (1992) 'The leakage of foreign exchange earnings from tourism', *Travel and Tourism Analyst* 3: 52–66.

Economist Intelligence Unit (various years) International Tourism Reports on various countries, London: *Economist* Intelligence Unit.

European Commission (1992) *The Future Development of the Common Transport Policy*, Brussels: European Union.

Global Aviation (1991) *Free Trade in the Air: An International Think-tank Report*, Washington, D.C.: Global Aviation Associates.

International Air Transport Association (1990) *The Economic Benefits of Air Transport*, Geneva: IATA.

International Air Transport Association (1992a) *Air Transport in a Changing World*, IATA White Paper, Geneva: IATA.

International Air Transport Association (1992b) *World Air Transport Statistics* 36, Geneva: IATA.

International Air Transport Association, Aviation Regulatory Watch Group (various years) *Annual Reports*, Geneva: IATA.

International Chamber of Commerce (1993) *Tourism, Regional Development and Bilateral Air Transport Negotiations*, Paris: ICC.

International Civil Aviation Organisation (1988) *Digest of Bilateral Air Transport Agreements*, Doc. 9511, Montreal: ICAO.

International Union of Official Tourism Organisations (1973) *Economic Aspects and Interdependence of International Tourism and Air Transport*, Madrid: IUOTO (now the World Tourism Organization).

Kasper, Daniel (1988) *Deregulation and Globalisation*, Cambridge, Mass.: Ballinger.

Middleton, Victor (1988) *Marketing in Travel and Tourism*, Oxford: Heinemann.

Naveau, Jacques (1989) *International Air Transport in a Changing World*, Brussels: Nijhoff.

Organisation for Economic Co-operation and Development (1993) *International Air Transport: The Challenges Ahead*, Paris: OECD.

Seekings, Kate (1993) *The Politics of Tourism*, London: Tourism International.

Waters, Somerset (1992) *Travel Industry World Yearbook* 36, New York: Child & Waters.

Wheatcroft, Stephen, and Lipman, Geoffrey (1986) *Air Transport in a Competitive European Market*, London: *Economist* Intelligence Unit.

Wheatcroft, Stephen and Lipman, Geoffrey (1989) *South Pacific Aviation and Tourism Policies for the Nineties*, Canberra: Australian Tourism Industry Association.

Wheatcroft, Stephen, and Lipman, Geoffrey (1990) *European Liberalisation and World Air Transport*, London: *Economist* Intelligence Unit.

Witt, Stephen, and Moutinho, Luiz (1989) *Tourism Marketing and Management Handbook*, London: Prentice Hall.

World Tourism Organization (1992) *Compendium of Tourism Statistics*, twelfth edition, Madrid: WTO.

World Tourism Organization (1992) *Tourism and the Environment*, Technical Series, Madrid: WTO.

World Travel and Tourism Council (1992) *Travel and Tourism in the World Economy*, Brussels: WTTC.

World Travel and Tourism Council (1993) *The Way Forward: Multilateral Air Transport Liberalisation*, Brussels: WTTC.

World Travel and Tourism Council (1993) *Travel and Tourism: A new Economic Perspective*, Brussels: WTTC.

Index

subsidies, protection against 20; *see also* protectionism
Sudan 87
Swissair/Switzerland 32, 33, 57
synergies and conflicts 1, 8–15; *see also* conflicts; growth
System One 33

TAESA (airline) 86
Taiwan 9, 13, 89
tariffs 14, 50; case studies 84, 91, 94; cheaper *see* charter operations; regulated 24–5, 37, 49
TAT (airline) 34
technological advance 14, 32–3, 81
Thai International 89
Thailand 61; liberalisation success 6, 65–6, 79, 88–9
'Third Package' 2, 28, 37, 76
tour operators *see* charter operations
tourism *see* aviation and tourism
Tradewinds (airline) 33
traffic rights: royalties for 25; *see also* sovereignty
transnational/multinational airlines 3, 27, 35, 78; *see also* multilateral agreements
Tropical Seas Air 89
Turkey 13, 61; charter boom 56, 68–9, 70–1, 79, 92, 93
Turks and Caicos 51
TWA (airline) 33, 57
'Two Airlines' policy (Australia) 83

unemployment 40
United Airlines 57; and changing aviation industry 30, 31, 32, 33
United Kingdom 57; and case studies 62, 68, 75, 84–5, 93, 100, 103, 104; changing aviation industry 28, 31, 33, 34–5, 37;

liberalisation and deregulation 28; regulation 19; *see also* British Airways
United Nations: Statistical Commission 40; *see also* International Civil Aviation Organization
United States 14, 57; and case studies 62–4, 85–7, 94; changing aviation industry 28–9, 30–7; liberalisation and deregulation 28–9; and Mexico 62–4, 85–7; regulation 19, 21, 24–5; synergies and conflicts 14
Uruguay *see* Mercosur
Uruguay Round of GATT 36
USAir 33, 34, 57
UTA (airline) 31

value added 40
Venezuela 34; protectionism, lingering 67, 91
Viasa (airline) 34
Virgin Islands, US 9, 13, 43

wages: household *see under* incomes; low, protection against 20; *see also* protectionism
White Paper (Brazil) 67, 90
World Bank 40, 100–1
World Tourism Organization i, ix–x, 80; and charter operations 70–1; Standard Industrial Classification of Tourism Activities 3, 40, 81; and synergies and conflicts 9, 10–14, 61; and tourism policies 3, 40, 42
Worldspan system 33

Yamoussoukro Declaration 68, 92
Yugoslavia 43